Life in the Victorian Kitchen

LIFE IN THE
VICTORIAN KITCHEN

Culinary Secrets and Servants' Stories

Karen Foy

PEN & SWORD
HISTORY

First published in Great Britain in 2014 by
Pen & Sword History
an imprint of
Pen & Sword Books Ltd
47 Church Street
Barnsley
South Yorkshire
S70 2AS

ISBN 978 1 78303 639 4

A CIP catalogue record for this book is available from the British
Library

Typeset in Ehrhardt by
Mac Style, Bridlington, East Yorkshire
Printed and bound in the UK by CPI Group (UK) Ltd,
Croydon, CRO 4YY

Pen & Sword Books Ltd incorporates the imprints of Pen &
Sword Archaeology, Atlas, Aviation, Battleground, Discovery,
Family History, History, Maritime, Military, Naval, Politics,
Railways, Select, Transport, True Crime, and Fiction, Frontline
Books, Leo Cooper, Praetorian Press, Seaforth Publishing and
Wharncliffe.

For a complete list of Pen & Sword titles please contact
PEN & SWORD BOOKS LIMITED
47 Church Street, Barnsley, South Yorkshire, S70 2AS, England
E-mail: enquiries@pen-and-sword.co.uk
Website: www.pen-and-sword.co.uk

Contents

Introduction

Have you ever read an old recipe, or an inherited family cookbook and wondered how your ancestors managed long before the introduction of the microwave and freezer? Just how should you 'coddle' an egg, how would you source a pineapple in the 1800s and what on earth was mock turtle soup? Today, we rarely take seasonal cooking into consideration, but long before the development of the modern supermarket, the availability of produce and ingredients dominated people's lives.

Picture the scene: it's a hot summer's day and fields of corn sway gracefully in the gentle mid-afternoon breeze, as jewel coloured kingfishers watch the world go by from the riverbank. Outside a tumbledown cottage children play, skipping alongside the vegetable patch, chasing each other between the lines of freshly laundered washing, whilst the aroma of hot fresh-baked bread wafts through the open kitchen window. Add appropriate costumes and a dash of makeup and you could have walked onto the set of a television period drama.

Even before TV gave us historical adaptations, our forebears often romanticised life in the past through paintings, which presented a highly idealised view of the world. These images of rural life, where the mother of a brood of children casually bakes bread on the kitchen table, seem carefree and easy – a moment in time captured on canvas. I often wish we could revisit the same scene half an hour later to see the reality: the mother up to her armpits in washing, with the stone floor to be scrubbed, the fire to be stoked, and the ongoing dilemma of feeding eight with only one loaf of bread.

Although these artists secured rose-tinted snapshots of an era before the camera, the reality was often harsh and unforgiving. Summers in the Victorian countryside, uninterrupted by industry and bursting with the sights and sounds of nature must have been glorious, but what about the bleak winters, when fields of frostbitten crops brought little work for the menfolk, leaving their families hungry?

Period novels help to give us further perspective, enabling us to revel in the luxurious lives of the wealthy whilst feeling grateful that we are not exposed to the dire situations experienced by the poor. Jane Austen largely avoids the subject of poverty in her novels and when she refers to the servants they rarely speak for themselves or reveal their thoughts and feelings, only confirming the belief that at this time domestics were 'seen and not heard'. Jane showcased polite society in her upper middle class tales of Regency life but, as the Victorian era dawned, writers began to give a truer picture of the wildly differing living conditions experienced among the social classes.

Dickens offers a glimpse of the underbelly of nineteenth century society and criticises the blind eye turned to it by the wealthy. Flora Thompson wrote of her late Victorian Oxfordshire childhood in what now seems like a rural idyll, yet behind the everyday occurrences she skilfully exposes the hardships faced by the hamlet dwellers compared to their contemporaries in the nearby town.

During this period, the lives of the rich and the poor could not have been more different. Their homes, amenities, employment choices and incomes were poles apart. In the nineteenth century, your social status determined everything from the way you wore your clothes to the food you ate. Etiquette was essential among the educated upper classes, but the working classes didn't have the time to linger over a leisurely breakfast. Employment was hard to come by and easily lost, so getting to work on time was their priority. They didn't possess multiple sets of cutlery, taking up a fresh one for each course, instead a single knife, fork and spoon for each family member.

For most ordinary working people, meals consisted of one simple course to deliberate over, and they could only dream of the lavish, exotically flavoured dishes enjoyed by the upper classes. Few had access to expensive ingredients, or the wherewithal to pay for them. Country people would sow basic crops in their small kitchen gardens or on a rough patch of land near their cottage and hope to grow enough produce to last the winter. Life was a constant battle of finding work, putting food on the table, clothing their families and maintaining their homes and, on the rare occasion when they had a spare half an hour, they had very little resources to do anything with it.

But every social class shared one common denominator. No matter what era we live in, our lives revolve around food – what we eat, when we eat, the quantity of our food, or the lack of it. As a result, the kitchen has long been the heart of every home, whether a basic cooking pot in a rural cottage or the bustling hub of a country mansion.

To fully understand the development of the Victorian kitchen, we must first look back at the economic history of Britain and the inherited legacy left by previous generations. From the battle to reduce the global price of wheat to the introduction of new labour-saving methods and innovations, each event, incident and invention revolutionised life within the home. The Victorians witnessed more rapid changes in mechanisation than in any previous era. Cooking over an open grate was commonplace at the start of Queen Victoria's reign, but when her era drew to a close, gas and electric devices, ground-breaking technology, and an endless variety of ingredients from the Empire had opened up a new and exciting culinary world to the British public.

Chapter One

The Rural Revolution: Feast and Famine

Oats: A grain, which in England is generally given to horses, but in Scotland supports the people.
   (Samuel Johnson, *A Dictionary of the English Language*, 1755)

When Queen Victoria came to the throne in 1837, Britain was in the midst of one of the many transitional periods that were to take place during her reign. Working the land remained one of the most common ways for Britons to earn a living, yet with compulsory education still far off on the horizon, a quarter of the population was living in poverty, with 40 per cent of the country's wealth owned by 5 per cent of the population. Britain was still feeling the effects of a war that had ended 20 years previously. The Napoleonic Wars had made it impossible to import corn from Europe, resulting in the expansion of British wheat farming and, for the landowner and farmer, an era of advancing progress and affluence.

Corn cultivation was on the increase. There had been huge improvements in machinery and farming implements: fields had been divided into a convenient workable size; drainage had been innovated; roads had been constructed and farm buildings erected. Investments were free-flowing and profits were rising, but for labourers and farm servants rents were rising and bread prices were soaring.

When the Napoleonic conflicts finally ended in 1815, it had been feared that foreign corn imports would lower grain prices, so British landowners appealed to the House of Commons to protect the profits of their farmers. The first of the Corn Laws was introduced stating that no foreign corn would be allowed into Britain until domestic corn reached a price of 80 shillings per quarter. Although landowners benefited from this decree, among the working classes this move was devastating. Artificially high corn prices meant that the bulk of their wages would be spent on bread. With little money left for workers to spend on other goods, manufacturing suffered, workers were laid off and slowly the economy began to decline.

Not to be beaten, the manufacturers and industrialists continued their campaign to extend the right to vote and be better represented in Parliament, gaining a say in the running of the country. A victory of sorts came with the Reform Act of 1832, which extended the right to vote to a large proportion of the industrial merchant classes. The legislation enabled their opinions and grievances to be officially recognised, yet little improvements were seen by the working classes until Prime Minister Robert Peel took up the challenge. Despite strong opposition, Peel considered the objections of the Anti-Corn Law League, the series of poor harvests and outbreaks of social unrest, as well as the Potato Famine then decimating the population of Ireland. Peel agreed that the restrictions on foreign corn imports were causing an unnecessary tax on food and a hindrance to British exports.

Eventually, in June 1846, the Corn Laws were abolished for good. There was initial uncertainty when landowners and agriculturalists believed they would no longer be able to command decent prices for their produce, yet their worries were short-lived and the farming economy continued to thrive. The repeal of the Corn Laws was a watershed moment in British history. After a long period of lucrative farming, the balance of power had gradually begun to shift from the landed gentry to the industrialists. The beginning of the nineteenth century was still dominated by agriculture and manpower, but within 40 years industry would begin to overshadow it.

By the 1870s, Britain was once more undergoing a period of agricultural adversity. There was very little expenditure on land improvement, as interest in farming ventures declined. Rapid growth of factories and industry in the preceding decades meant there were fewer areas available for arable cultivation. The Tithe Commutation Survey estimated that wheat made up 26.8 per cent of the crops grown in England and Wales in 1836. By 1871, the Annual Agricultural Returns saw this figure drop to 23 per cent, with a steady decline to 16 per cent by 1911.

Previously, Britain had depended upon home-grown produce but soon the country was no longer as reliant on its rural economy. The arrival of the railways brought faster transportation, while steam power and new innovations allowed larger scale production. Wheat prices fell rapidly from 55 shillings to 28 shillings a quarter between 1870 and 1890.

The effects of these mammoth changes were felt by everyone – from the lowest paid labourer in a two-room cottage to the wealthiest aristocrat in a stately mansion.

Living off the Land

During the nineteenth century, the Poor Law Commissioners divided parishes into two types. 'Open' parishes consisted of villages where houses were owned by small-scale landlords and occupied by many agricultural labourers, while within 'Close' parishes, villages were dominated by landlords and ratepayers and tended to exclude the poor, who were viewed as a drain on the local resources. A perfect example of this division is captured in Flora Thompson's *Lark Rise to Candleford*, where the labourers living in the small hamlet of Lark Rise take the long daily walk to Candleford, the nearest town, to find work.

The second official census, taken in March 1851, provided a picture of the economic status of mid-Victorian England and Wales. It showed that over 1.4 million people – approximately 23 per cent of working men – were employed on the land as farmers, agricultural labourers, or farm servants. Alongside them were female relatives of the farmers and children under the age of 15, who also had their roles to play. Although their work was not always recorded on the census, they too laboured in the fields, helping with the harvest by following the reapers and binding the sheaves of corn.

The Hon Edward Stanhope investigated the employment of women and children in agriculture in the late 1860s. His observations, submitted to the Royal Commissioners, help us to understand the feelings of labouring country men, who found it difficult to tolerate their wives and daughters working the land, seeing it as a humiliation.

> The woman takes her part in the coarseness of the fields. Her presence is no restraint on language. She becomes in all but sex a man among the men. Those husbands and brothers who have the finest instincts among the labourers, feel it a deep degradation, even when they must submit to it, that their wives and sisters have to work in the fields.

There was a strict hierarchy between the farmer and his workforce, although the distinction between labourer and farm servant was not always well defined. Farm servants were often young boys in their mid-teens or unmarried men, hired at a local fair on a yearly basis, or employed privately through word-of-mouth recommendations. Agricultural labourers and skilled workers, such as shepherds, ploughmen, herdsmen and hedge cutters, were usually married and employed either on a casual basis or as regular workers. When hired, their abilities, previous employment and family circumstances would be taken into account before a wage was offered.

Landowning farmers often found it beneficial to provide rented cottages for their workers. Known as 'tied housing', the accommodation was tied to the job and when an employee left, or was no longer required, he and his family had to move out. For the labourer this could be quite a precarious position. Having a roof over their heads deterred them from complaining about poor conditions, ill-treatment or low wages, in case their objections led to their eviction. It was essential for the worker to prove themselves hard-working and indispensable, as there was no guarantee of employment and little security as labourers grew old and infirm. The worker was at the mercy of the good nature and charity of their employer.

Labourers who remained on the same farm or estate for a long period, raised their families and, in turn, a new generation of farm workers, with the tied cottage often passing down to the eldest son upon the death of the labourer. Imbued with the knowledge of farming life from an early age, they became highly-skilled workers who knew the lay of the land and the challenges of nature. Daughters started on the employment ladder as bird scarers and 'gleaners', collecting left-over corn and vegetables in the fields after a harvest, before taking on a labouring role or a more skilled position in the dairy as a milkmaid or domestic servant in their employer's house.

The milk maid would usually milk the cows twice a day. In the morning she would sieve and cool the milk ready to sell, whilst the milk collected during the evening would be used to make butter and cheese. Specific days would be set aside for the long, laborious processes involved in butter and cheese-making, but throughout her working week she would be expected to monitor the welfare of the animals, keep the dairy clean and the milking pails scrubbed and scalded with boiling water ready for the next milking.

A busy farm would often require a domestic known as a 'maid of all work'. Her day would start at dawn when she prepared the range for cooking. Any other fires within the home were lit, water heated and taken upstairs to enable the family to wash – all before she began the task of organising breakfast. In the morning, soups and stews were prepared for later in the day, whilst her additional list of chores might include scrubbing the kitchen floor, washing the laundry, making beds and mending garments. These women worked as hard as their male counterparts on the farm; their days were long with a constant stream of tasks to be completed before they could contemplate going to bed.

Case Study: The Life of a Victorian Farm Labourer

Warwickshire-born Joseph Arch was the son of a farm labourer. At the age of nine he started work as a bird-scarer on a local smallholding, the first step towards developing his agricultural skills. When he later became a Methodist lay preacher, Joseph acquired a reputation for championing the concerns of the farm labourer. Joseph's biography vividly recalls how his family was affected by the Corn Laws and the difficulties they faced just to get a simple meal on the table:

It was 1835, the winter of the Repeal of the Corn Laws. I was about nine years old. I well remember eating barley bread, and seeing the tears in my poor mother's eyes as she cut slices off a loaf ... It was a terrible winter ...

There was corn enough for everybody, that was the hard, cruel part of it but those who owned it would not sell it out when it was sorely needed. They kept it back, they locked it up; and all the time the folk were crying out in their extremity for bread ... To make as much money as they could, by letting corn rise to famine prices, was all the owners of it cared about. "Make money at any price" was their motto.

Meat was rarely, if ever, to be seen on the labourer's table; the price was too high for his pocket ... In many a household even a morsel of bacon was considered a luxury. Flour was so dear that the cottage loaf was mostly of barley.

The Victorian Vegetable Patch

The nineteenth century domestic cook was constrained by the seasons and the availability of produce grown locally. As a rule, approximately one eighth of an acre (or 20 rods, as the measurement was then known) was expected to feed a family of five. This would provide enough space to grow vegetables – potatoes, cabbages, onions, leeks, carrots, beans and parsnips – with an area set aside to keep a pig, chickens or ducks. Some householders had the luxury of keeping a cow, providing them with milk to make their own butter and cheese.

The extra food grown in the vegetable garden often ensured a family's survival, so every last inch of space was utilised, with fruit trees trained against the walls of the cottage and small bushes planted on spare patches of land to provide berries.

In the countryside, many families had access to a patch of land surrounding their cottage upon which they could grow food, but plenty of others who lacked this facility, were known as 'landless labourers'. Parliament was keen to promote allotments among the working classes to solve this problem and the creation of an Allotment Movement was outlined in parliamentary papers and the reports of the Board of Agriculture. The Society for Bettering the Conditions and Increasing the Comforts of the Poor was founded in the late eighteenth century, but the project was slow to gain support. However, after a series of harvest failures and the growth in the number of landless labourers, the early plots provided a model for a larger venture and between 1829 and 1873 England saw one allotment created for every three male agricultural labourers. At the end of this period, over 240,000 allotments had been established, giving these workers the opportunity to feed their families without having to rely on poor relief.

Labourers worked their allotments in the same way any cottager planted his kitchen garden. The principles were also the same used by any farmer, but applied on a much smaller scale, with allotments ranging in size from half a rod to a quarter of an acre. A great deal of thought was given to the type of produce grown, whether planting mainstay vegetables such as potatoes, onions, carrots, cabbages and kale or training climbers like broad beans up against a wall or bordering hedgerow.

With the main part of an allotment devoted to a system of regularly rotated kitchen crops, much emphasis was put upon the preparation and the type of manure used to ensure a successful harvest. The Victorians were keen recyclers. An article in Mrs Beeton's *All About Gardening* (1871) advised: 'The droppings of cattle, sheep, pigs, and all house sewage, should be collected and saved, and mixed with rather more than the same quantity of garden soil: the application of a little quicklime will remove any offensive smell'.

Many local varieties of vegetables were grown in allotments and cottage gardens. Types of peas, for instance, included Emperor, Bishop's Long Pod and Blue Imperials – although not everyone chose to grow peas, as the harvest was small for the amount of room required to grow them. Silver Globe onions, Kirk's Kidney potatoes, early Dutch turnips, Ragged Jack Kale and Colewort cabbages were also highly rated. Herbs – considered essential to add to stocks, stews and soups as well as providing medicinal relief – could be grown in any small corner. Rhubarb was easy to cultivate and provided a plentiful harvest, whilst those with sufficient room might decide to plant fruit trees or bushes. The choice of apples at this time was endless, from the Blenheim Orange to the Kerry Pippin. Greengage and Victoria plums were popular along with Kentish cherries, Lancashire Hero gooseberries and Falstaff raspberries.

Where possible, crops were rotated on a yearly cycle to ensure high yields, and planning was needed to decide where specific varieties would flourish; some crops required shelter from frost, whilst others benefited from being planted in a sunny position. Just like the farmer, the country cottager and allotment-holder was at the mercy of the seasons and needed to ensure that the best use was made of their land to enable a wide selection of produce to be harvested throughout the year.

Whilst crops such as radishes and lettuce could be grown in a matter of weeks, others took months to reach maturity. No sooner had the onions been grown, dried, and taken into the kitchen ready to be used, than the patch of land in which they had been raised would be dug over and replaced with a different crop. Certain flowers, such as marigolds and lavender, were planted in-between each variety, not only to look pretty, but also to act as natural pesticides and deter the bugs from eating the crops.

Weather conditions, planting times, harvesting and the benefits of eating certain produce were often dictated by folklore and traditional rhymes passed down within families. Some warned to, 'Eat leeks in March and wild garlic in May, and all year after physicians may play', while others forecast, 'Mist in May, heat in June, makes a harvest come right soon', or 'A cold May is kindly, and fills the barn finely'.

In a classic prophesy for the end of the year, all apparently depended upon the direction of the wind:

> *If on New Year's Eve night the wind blow south,*
> *It betokeneth warmth and growth;*
> *If west, much milk, and fishes in the sea;*
> *If north, much cold and storms there will be;*
> *If east, the trees will bear much fruit;*
> *If north-east, flee it, man and brute!*

When harvests were good, the Victorian cottager had an extremely healthy diet, but poor seasons and lack of money could change their fortunes virtually overnight. Even within working class communities there were varying states of existence, and bad harvests could have a devastating effect on individual families. At such times, the humble potato provided a reliable source of sustenance. It was relatively easy to grow, bulked out a meal when there was little or no meat available, and was perfect for baking in the grate, ready to carry out to workers in the fields at lunch time.

The importance of the potato in the diet of working people can be seen in the example of the Irish Potato famine during the 1840s. It is said that Sir Walter Raleigh planted the first potatoes in Ireland on his 40,000 acre estate near Cork, attempting to debunk the myth that they were poisonous. Whatever the truth of this, during the seventeenth century Irish peasants realised the numerous benefits of cultivating the vegetable, from its ability to grow in poor soil to the ease with which it could be stored. It was wholesome and sustaining and soon became an essential part of the Irish diet. Poor families enhanced meals consisting of this staple crop with cabbage, salt or fish.

As growing potato crops in poor soil freed space for more profitable wheat, landowners encouraged their tenants to produce the crop. Potato planting would begin in the spring, usually around St Patrick's Day, and harvests were reaped in September. July and August were often the lean months when the previous year's harvest was beginning to run out and workers had to turn to highly priced oats and barley to form the basis of their meals.

Sadly, the Irish dependency on the potato had disastrous results. In September 1845, a major outbreak of potato blight swept through Europe. The plants turned black and curly and soon began to rot. It was later discovered that an airborne fungus, transported from the hulks of ships travelling from North America to England, had swept across the fields of Ireland causing devastation. The fungal spores thrived in the moist conditions, settling on the plants and multiplying to infect thousands of others within days. With their food source literally eliminated overnight, people quickly began to starve.

The famine led to over one million deaths, causing those who could afford to pay for their passage to flee the country in search of a better life in England, Australia, New Zealand, Canada or America. Known as the Irish Diaspora, this mass movement of people meant that the population of Ireland decreased by two million between 1847 and 1851. Today, it is hard to believe that the potato completely changed the face of a nation, but this vegetable once caused a disaster that touched all Victorian Britons.

Chapter Two

The Heart of the Home:
Inside the Cottage Kitchen

There are people in the world so hungry, that God cannot appear to them except in the form of bread.

(Charles Dickens, *Oliver Twist*, 1838)

Whilst the men spent their days labouring in the fields and around the farm, many Victorian countrywomen spent most of their time working in the kitchen. There the food was prepared and eaten, the laundry washed, ironed and mended, and the children entertained. Compared with today's modern workspaces, the mid-Victorian cottage kitchen was a basic affair. The walls were rough brick or lime washed, whilst the only soft furnishings gracing the bare wooden floorboards or cold stone floor might be a small rag rug.

Rag rugs were created in the evenings using scraps of old fabrics from worn-out clothes, which were poked through a backing cloth using a skewer of bone or horn, to make a simple pile. This lack of floor covering also reflected the hard wear and tear the kitchen floor received, with the constant tread of dirty boots, dripping clothes and cooking spillages; it needed to be swept at least twice a day.

It is important to note that this would also have been the only room in the house heated by an open wood fire, or range, and this was another incentive for the family to spend most of their time there. For those able to afford one, the range consisted of a cast iron fire/oven combination, requiring black lead polishing on a regular basis to keep it clean. Lit every morning, it took a while to reach a high enough temperature to provide water hot enough for washing and cooking. Several family members might be spending long hours working the land, so soups and stews were prepared. Left to simmer away on top of the stove or over the fire, they provided a hot meal no matter what time the workers returned home. The residual heat from the range warmed the room so the kitchen would often be covered by wet clothes which could not be hung out to dry in the winter months, or on rainy days.

Before the introduction of gas lighting, candles – made from beeswax, or tallow, a rendered form of beef or mutton fat – rush lights and oil lamps were the only means of illuminating cottages once darkness fell. Trimming wicks and preparing oil lamps was just one of the many jobs on a housewife's long list of chores. Perhaps surprisingly, rush lights were still in use in rural England right up to the end of the nineteenth century. With 20 sold for a penny, their light was dim, yet steady. Households could make these artificial lights themselves by soaking the dry pith of the rush plant in grease or fat, before igniting it for a soft glow. William Corbett, an English farmer, journalist and staunch opposer of the Corn Laws, commented that, 'this rush light cost almost nothing to produce and was believed to give a better light than some poorly dipped candles'.

The annual Medieval tradition of performing 'rush bearing ceremonies' continued well into the Victorian era, before declining in popularity towards the end of the nineteenth century. This custom required rushes to be gathered and strewn over the earthen or cold stone floors of the church, to purify the air with their sweet aroma.

Rural families often had very little in the way of decoration for their homes, so would retain images from illustrated newspapers to adhere to the walls. In the BBC adaptation of *Lark Rise to Candleford*, this practice has been captured perfectly in the cottage kitchen of the Timmins family. By the late 1880s, mass production put novelty items and ornaments within the reach of the working man's wage and so small trinkets, and later, perhaps even a clock began to be displayed around the home.

In June 1893, long after the Corn Laws had been abolished, Maud Morrison, a writer for *The Girl's Own Paper*, imagined an idyllic cottager's life in Sussex:

My wants ... are very few, and except flour and a little grocery, the cows, poultry, and garden supply all our food. An array of beehives, twenty or thirty of them, painted of diverse colours, stand among the fruit trees. These I manage entirely myself but ... have help ... in straining, bottling and packing the honey for market.

The villagers have almost given up gleaning now, bread is so cheap; but we find that it decidedly lightens our bill for poultry food. Wheat, oats, barley – nothing comes amiss to the fowls; and the straw goes into the pigsty.

She notes that animals are fed on leftovers: 'Two little black pigs, eagerly devour a supper of potato parings, and such scraps boiled in buttermilk'. Even the garden is well thought-out, providing food for both family and livestock. Alongside 'large strawberry beds ... a good sized plot was devoted to Mangold Worzel for the cow's winter provender, and between the rows of potatoes were cabbages, newly planted for the same purpose'.

Maud highlights the need to keep poultry as, not only did they provide a regular supply of eggs, but once their laying days were numbered, the roasted bird would feed the family. Allowed to roam free within the garden, scratching in the dirt and living off seeds and scraps, a chicken was an essential purchase that would reward its owner with very little wastage.

The American novelist, Harriet Beecher Stowe's comic description of 'Aunt Chloe' in her 1852 novel *Uncle Tom's Cabin* must have applied to many a housewife when it was time for one of her fowls to meet their end:

> A cook she certainly was, in the very bone and centre of her soul. Not a chicken or turkey or duck in the barn-yard but looked grave when they saw her approaching, and seemed evidently to be reflecting on their latter end; and certain it was that she was always meditating on trussing, stuffing and roasting, to a degree that was calculated to inspire terror in any reflecting fowl living.

Despite this, the keeping of hens was surrounded with folklore and superstitions. 'Old beliefs die as hard as old practices, and in country places, not so very remote either, the most foolish and unfounded notions often flourish and are likely to flourish for many a day', wrote countryside expert, James Mason in an 1889 article on food folklore. Customs and superstition played a large part in the lives of our Victorian ancestors, and despite the era being known as a period of enlightenment, it is surprising how slow attitudes were to change.

As hens and their eggs were a vital part of the countryman's diet, much importance was placed upon them. Over in the West of Ireland it was believed that eggs laid on Good Friday would never go stale, whilst in some areas the first egg laid by a pullet was given to a young man to present to his sweetheart, in the belief that this was the luckiest gift he could give her. Those desiring to know more about their future, their likelihood of attaining wedded bliss, or the domestic skills of a potential wife also turned to a new-laid egg for an answer.

A noted Victorian expert on country customs, the Rev. Thomas Firminger Thistelton Dyer, explained the process of egg divination to those with a quest for knowledge:

perforate with a pin the small end of an egg, and let three drops of the white fall into a basin of water, which soon defuse themselves on the surface into a variety of fantastic shapes. From these the fortune teller will predict the fortunes of the credulous one ... the character ... and a variety of particulars concerning his domestic happiness.

Egg divination, known as 'Oomancy', was performed not only in Victorian Britain, but also in many other cultures around the world. The methods carried out to complete each type of egg reading were passed down within families and used to find answers to physical or medical problems. The occult nature of the prediction injected an element of fear into the results forecast.

A news item reported in the *Stamford Mercury* of October 1852 reveals the extent to which some Victorian country folk adhered to superstitions surrounding eggs. The reporter tells 'the tale of a person in want of some eggs', who had called one evening at a farmhouse in East Markham. The visitor asked the woman of the house if she had any eggs to sell, and she replied that she had a few scores to dispose of, to which the man asked if he could take them with him.

She answered, 'You are welcome to the eggs at a proper hour of the day; but I would not let them go out of the house after the sun is set on any consideration whatsoever'. This strange reasoning originated from the conviction that it was a bad omen to bring eggs in or out of the house after dark.

The giving of eggs at Easter also has an important spiritual connotation. Religious festivals and gatherings were an integral part of Victorian life, with annual fêtes marking notable dates throughout the countryside calendar. At Easter, Christians believed that the egg represented the future, as a symbol of the Resurrection. In the days after the abstinence of Lent was over and festivities began, eggs were decoratively stained in a variety of colours and distributed as an emblem of the return of life after death.

The Victorians continued the traditions of their forebears, and despite their forward-thinking ideals, retained strong beliefs in the mystical. Accepted by Victorians from all walks of life, a whole variety of superstitions were deemed to predict a believer's fortune, fate and future. For the country-dweller, not only the egg was capable of revealing important answers to their questions, but the behaviour of the chickens also had the potential to provide guidance.

In Scotland, it was said that 'whistling maids and crowing hens are no canny about a house', the sentiment thought to suggest that masculine qualities in a woman were not desirable; an attitude shared in France, where a crowing hen is considered unlucky. Cock crowing was thought to signify a warning and, along with announcing the break of dawn, it was believed to banish any ghosts, fiends or sprites. Even Shakespeare wrote about this phenomenon when his ghost in *Hamlet* 'faded at the crowing of the cock'. This tradition was particularly welcome at Christmas, when a crowing cock would drive away any malignant spirits and signal a peaceful start to the year ahead. Held in high regard, the cockerel symbolised protection; keeping evil at bay, its image was often used to adorn the tops of church steeples to 'watch over' the congregation within.

How to 'Coddle' Your Eggs

Working class Victorians enjoyed their eggs simply boiled or poached, but in middle and upper class families, a 'coddled' egg was often preferred. Coddling, a method similar to poaching, allowed an egg to be cooked very briefly and enabled the yolk to stay soft. Beautifully decorated egg coddlers, in the form of small pots with tight-fitting lids, were commercially produced by nineteenth century pottery and kitchenware manufacturers. The coddler was smeared with butter and the egg poured gently into it, before being lowered into a pot of boiling water for five to six minutes. The coddled egg was then eaten directly from the pot or slid on to a plate and served – often for breakfast – with small pieces of bacon, salmon flakes and other savoury items.

Despite the majority of the Victorian household income being spent on food, the variety of food consumed by many was minimal. A few ounces of tea, sugar, cheese, and a small amount of meat and vegetables comprised the daily menu for most, with bread making up the bulk of the meal. Bread has been the focus of our lives for hundreds of years and, whilst compiling her recipe book *Modern Cookery for Private Families* in 1845, even Eliza Acton had to admit: 'Without wishing in the slightest degree to disparage the skill and labour of bread makers by trade, truth compels us to assert our conviction of the superior wholesomeness of bread made in our own homes'. In short, fresh home-baked bread tasted better.

For our ancestors, bread was simple to make and only required four ingredients – flour, water, salt and yeast – yet many families' lives revolved around earning enough money to buy the flour, then bake their bread, before the cycle started all over again. The cost of bread was the most important item in a family's weekly budget, yet during the nineteenth century bread prices fluctuated considerably.

Initially, the Napoleonic Wars had made it impossible to import corn from Europe. To rectify this Britain had expanded her wheat farming ventures, but in doing so the price of bread rocketed. Legislation was passed in the form of the Corn Laws, which favoured the landowning farmers, increasing their profits at the expense of the general public, who were paying greatly inflated prices for a single loaf. When the Irish potato crop failed in 1845, the government was forced to reconsider their decision to boost wheat prices, as thousands of people succumbed to famine and starvation. In 1846, the duty on oats, barley and wheat was reduced to one shilling per quarter, which had a significant knock-on effect on the prices paid by the consumer.

Wheat prices may have fluctuated, but Britain still required a way of processing the crop into flour. 'Earning a crust' is a term still used to describe the act of working to acquire a wage that derives from the early nineteenth century, when hundreds of thousands of people were employed as millers, millwrights, engineers and milling craftsmen. Despite this extensive workforce stretching the length and breadth of Britain, when mechanised milling methods were introduced during the Industrial Revolution the demand for cheaper white bread saw the gradual demise of the traditional mill.

A Baker's Dozen

Buying flour from the local miller allowed women to bake their own loaves at home, while those living and working in towns and cities usually bought bread direct from a baker. We have all heard the term a 'Baker's Dozen', referring to a quantity of 13 rather than the usual 12 in a dozen, but did you know its origins?

As far back as the twelfth century, the price at which bakers sold their bread was regulated according to the price of wheat. By the 1850s, the government was well aware of the importance of bread in the nation's diet, so the penalty was severe for bakers cheating customers with short measures or bulking them out with additives. Fines were known to have been imposed, short prison terms issued, and even transportation to Australia was considered for those flouting the law. For fear of incurring any penalties, bakers added an extra loaf when selling batches of 12 loaves, to make 13, giving us our phrase a 'Baker's Dozen'.

The Victorian Pantry

Before the invention of the refrigerator, the pantry reigned supreme in both humble cottage kitchens and in the large scale kitchens of great stately homes. The pantry was a walk-in store cupboard, with a stone floor and stone or slate shelves, which helped to keep perishable items cool. The low temperature ensured that the food inside remained as fresh as possible, even on a hot sunny day. If the pantry was large enough to accommodate a small window, then this would be covered with a wire mesh to deter flies, yet still allow the air to circulate.

In modern fridge freezers we are aware of cross contamination and avoid placing raw food above or alongside cooked items to prevent the spread of bacteria. A similar method was used in the pantry, with the bottom shelf reserved for raw meat and the middle shelf for freshly-picked vegetables. The top shelves were used for dairy products, with a bowl for new-laid eggs, jugs of milk and cream covered with weighted, beaded cloths to keep the flies at bay, and an area set aside for pats of butter. This was often made with milk from the family's own cow, churned outside the cottage door and paddled into shape on the kitchen table. A wedge of cheese might be found nestling beneath a lidded ceramic dish – a staple food to accompany home-baked bread and a slice of home-grown onion. Cooked foods, such as pies and pastries, and a bread bin, covered with a lid to keep the bread fresh, would also occupy this area.

Depending upon the size of this store cupboard, it may have housed extra wooden shelves, where home-made preserves, pickles and bottled fruits and sauces could be kept, alongside dry ingredients, such as flour, salt and sugar which would have been needed on a daily basis. Hooks were screwed into the ceiling of the pantry to enable cooked hams to be stored out of the way. These were also useful for suspending game birds. With so much effort going into smoking, salting and preserving foods, it was important to create the right conditions to keep them in. It was essential to avoid dampness and condensation at all costs, and instead create a cool, dry environment to keep the supplies in the best condition possible.

Just like the kitchen garden, the well-stocked pantry also made good use of available space and, as the saying goes, in an organised household, there was 'a place for everything and everything in its place'. Pedlars, hucksters and gypsies travelled the country lanes, selling baskets and brushes on the doorstep. Many housewives used these baskets to store fruit, vegetables and grain on the floor of their pantry.

Vinegar: A Store Cupboard Favourite

For the Victorian cottager, shop-bought cleaning products were few and far between, but one simple home-made product had a myriad of uses: vinegar. The creation of vinegar does not require a detailed recipe with numerous steps to follow, as any liquid containing sugar will automatically turn to vinegar when exposed to air for a certain length of time. By leaving wine, fresh juices, or uncooked cider uncorked for about a week, the combination of alcohol in the liquid, bacteria and exposure to oxygen will trigger a chemical reaction, which provides us with vinegar in its simplest form.

By the nineteenth century, vinegar was essential for pickling and preserving vegetables, and as spices found their way into British homes, the addition of pepper, cayenne, and allspice only helped to infuse the mixture further. Its acidic qualities made it ideal for cleaning glass, removing stains and deodorising smells, forming an early kitchen sanitiser which could kill moulds and fungus, and ultimately destroy germs.

With very few medical supplies then available, a bottle of vinegar was not only a culinary favourite, but vital for family ailments. Its antiseptic qualities helped speed up the healing of wounds and soothed rashes and insect bites. When mixed with honey, vinegar was used as a cough suppressant and believed to dissolve warts. Herbal-infused concoctions were created using vinegar as a base to cure all manner of health problems. Some believed that a small tot of cider vinegar a day would even promote vigour and longevity.

Chapter Three

Country Matters

Pork – no animal is more used for nourishment and none more indispensable in the kitchen; employed either fresh or salt, all is useful, even to its bristles and its blood; it is the superfluous riches of the farmer, and helps to pay the rent of the cottager.

(Alexis Soyer, nineteenth century French chef,
The Modern Housewife, 1851)

To supplement their diet, many Victorian labourers kept a pig. The animal was an integral part of the cottager's life and would be kept in the yard, on a patch of land adjoining the cottage, or in a makeshift sty. There are even some instances when the pig was given space within the house. Living in close proximity to their animal, the whole family would take responsibility for its welfare. In autumn, the children would be sent out to collect acorns to enliven the pig's diet, and even neighbouring villagers who did not have their own beast, would contribute to its feed with scraps from their kitchens, in return for some of its meat when the animal was slaughtered.

The pig was primarily a source of meat not a pet, so slaughtering the pig was a reality of rural life. The animal would be fattened before slaughter in the late autumn and then smoked or salted to provide a meat source during the winter and spring. Thomas Hardy dedicated a whole chapter to this necessary act in his 1895 novel, *Jude the Obscure*.

The services of a pork butcher or 'pig sticker' were required to despatch the animal and the skill of the expert had a huge impact on how quickly and cleanly the pig was slaughtered. Born in the late 1890s, Northamptonshire cottager Sid Tyrell recollected the occasion: 'with a clumsy rough butcher there would be men shouting and a pig squealing for no end of time so that the entire village would know what was going on and the boys would come from all directions to see the gory spectacle'. But Sid only had words of praise for his own local pig sticker, who killed pigs 'in the most gentlemanly sort of way'.

In *Lark Rise to Candleford*, Flora Thompson recalled the brutality of a pig-killing which took place in her Oxfordshire village. 'The killing was a noisy, bloody business, the animal was hoisted to a rough bench that it might bleed thoroughly and so preserve the quantity of the meat'. The slaughter took place after dark, and she described how lanterns would provide light and a fire of burning straw would be lit to singe the bristles off the carcass of the animal. 'The whole scene, with its mud and blood, flaring lights and dark shadows was as savage as anything to be seen in an African jungle.'

Although Flora's childhood memories lingered into adulthood 'she was sorry for the pig ... as she stood alone in the pantry where the dead animal hung suspended from a hook in the ceiling,' children's author Beatrix Potter was not quite so sentimental. Three years after buying Hill Top Farm, she drafted a letter of protest against proposed legislation to make it 'illegal for a child of under sixteen years of age to be present at the slaughter and cutting up of carcasses'. Beatrix reminisced that one of her early memories was of 'helping to scrape the smiling countenance of my grandmother's deceased pig with scalding water and the sharp edged bottom of a brass candlestick'.

But once the horrors of despatching the pig had begun to fade, the preservation of the meat for the coming months began. Hams and bacons were salted and dried, lard was collected and the pig's intestines, known as chitterlings, were cleaned; pies were made and hog's puddings created from a mixture of pork meat, fat, suet, bread, and barley. The joy of eating the delicious meat was traditionally celebrated with a 'pig feast', which took place on the Sunday following the slaughter.

In later weeks, when it was time to eat the bacon, 'salamandering' – a unique cooking method described by Flora Thompson as 'peculiar to smithy families' – was carried out:

> Thin slices of bacon or ham were spread out on a large plate and taken to the smithy, where the plate was placed on the anvil. The (black) smith then heated red hot one end of a large, flat iron utensil known as the 'salamander' and held it above the plate until the rashers were crisp and curled.

Owning a pig was undoubtedly a huge bonus to a Victorian family, but if you had the wherewithal to keep a cow, then the benefits also extended to creating the by-products of its milk.

Cheese-making

For wealthy Victorian families cheese was just one of several courses at a meal, whilst for the poorer classes it was often the mainstay of a meal, inspiring the quote by author and food connoisseur Eugene Briffault, 'Cheese complements a good dinner and supplements a bad one'.

By the nineteenth century, cheese-making had been carried out in Britain for hundreds of years. Eleventh century monks helped to refine the techniques still used today. The processes used in making the traditional favourite, Wensleydale can be traced back to the twelfth century Cistercian monks at Jervaulx Abbey in Yorkshire. It soon became a tradition to name the cheese by the region in which it was made and by the early 1800s an assortment of cheeses were being produced in farmhouses across the United Kingdom.

Despite a long period of success for the British cheese industry, the Industrial Revolution and the development of the railways would have a huge impact on local cheese-making operations. Gradually, it became more profitable for dairymen to sell their milk on, rather than to use it to make cheese, as the efficiency of the rail network made transportation over longer distances much more viable.

As a rule, better quality milk meant better quality cheese. Factors such as the diet and the type of grass, hay or silage that the cattle had been fed upon all contributed to the taste of the finished product. Cheese was made by a process of separating the milk into the 'curds' or solids, and the 'whey' or liquid. Many different methods were used to begin this process – including the addition of lemon juice or vinegar to the milk to encourage separation. Perhaps the most common, which also guaranteed success and an edible cheese, was to use 'rennet', the natural enzyme which was found in a calf's stomach. By draining off the whey, which was used to feed the pigs, the curds could be milled, salted and packed in a cloth-lined mould, before being weighted in a press for approximately one week to squeeze out any excess moisture. The resulting cheese could then be left on a cool, dry shelf to mature.

Mentioned in the Domesday Book, Cheshire Cheese is Britain's oldest variety of cheese – a particular favourite at the court of Queen Elizabeth I, and Royal Navy ships were said to be stocked with it in the 1750s. Although it was originally aged to varying levels of hardness to withstand transportation from the country to the city by horse and cart, the crumbly texture we know today later became the preferred choice, requiring a shorter storage time during production and reducing the price of the final cheese.

Such was the importance of cheese-making in counties like Cheshire, that in the village of Peover it was said that if a girl wished to be a good farmer's wife she had to lift the lid of the parish chest one-handed before she was betrothed, in order to prove that she had the strength required for cheese making.

The parchment-covered journal of John Byram, a farmer who lived in Cheshire, creates an accurate picture of exactly how agriculture, farming and the kitchen were inextricably linked during the early to mid-Victorian period. A hefty one-inch thick, the book is filled with notes, clippings and recipes. Started on Lady Day in 1831 and covering over 50 years, it sheds light on the worries and wonders of a different world, also revealing how the life of a dairy farmer and cheese-maker revolved around his cattle.

> 1849 – 16 cows died of Pleura pneumonia. Began March 1st 1849 and continued till August 12th. Sold five off for £11. Lost in all 21 cows.

He then jots down a recipe that he hopes will cure any more outbreaks of the pneumonia:

John Morton's receipt for Pleura Pneumonia

2 oz Carbonate of Soda
4 oz Cream of Tartar
8 oz Sulphur

To be given … in 3 pints warm water.
Do not bleed or give much meal for two or three days.

John's notes constantly refer to the planting and harvesting of food crops essential for the family table, with numerous entries in the spring giving us an idea of the types of seeds he was sowing.

> March 19th 1863 – Onions and Radish.
> March 20th 1863 – Oats sown and Potatoes set.

However, the product from which he made most of his income was his cheese.

> 11th July 1853 – sold 40 cheese at Chester Fair to Thomas of Liverpool.

Such was John's pride in his cheese-making skills that he cut and pasted a clipping out of the newspaper into his journal. It reads:

Prize cheese made in 1857

The prize cheese for which John Byram, Pool Farm, Eastham received The Royal Agricultural Society's prize of £20 in July 1858, are on view and sale at T & R Bells, 58 St John's Market, Liverpool.

After numerous cheese sales and cattle bought and sold, one entry at the end of the book sums up John's agricultural career: 'Finished farming by the grace of God February 2nd 1871'. This gives the impression that he felt lucky to have survived this turbulent era of farming, having provided a sufficient income for his family.

Butter-making

In rural Britain, one of the necessary skills for nineteenth century countrywomen was butter-making. Using the cream from the milk and a little added salt, the process of butter-making was simple – all it took was time, energy and some basic equipment. The low-tech butter-making process was basically the same wherever it was carried out. The cows were milked by hand, usually twice a day, by the dairyman or milk maid. In the 1880s, without the aid of modern equipment, 200 gallons of milk could be collected per year from one cow. As the farming world developed and new machines were introduced, a century later, quantities had drastically changed and 1,000 gallons were expected from each cow.

Sitting on a small three-legged stool, the dairymaid would place a wooden bucket underneath the cow's udder to collect the liquid. Then, with the aid of the yoke – a wooden support laid across the shoulders, which took the weight of the containers hanging beneath – the buckets would be carried from the place of milking into the farmhouse, where this liquid was sieved into an earthenware crock pot to cool. During this rest period, the cream would rise to the top, allowing it to be easily skimmed off and separated from the milk. The cream would be poured into the butter churn and agitated with a wooden pounding stick, breaking down the fat membranes. The liquid fat, or buttermilk, was released and the remainder would 'cement' together to make a cream solid. Salt was also added to taste.

Churning butter could be a laborious process and many housewives would get their children to help. Reciting a popular old rhyme known as an 'Essex Charm for a Churn', the words are said to date back to 1650, according to Percy B. Green's *History of Nursery Rhymes,* published in 1899. Although originating from Essex, this traditional ditty was adopted by women across the country, to pass the time whilst churning and to encourage the butter to 'appear' from the milk:

> *Come, butter, come; Come, butter, come,*
> *Peter stands at the gate*
> *Waiting for his buttered cake,*
> *Come, butter, come.*

Folklore and superstition also surrounded the butter-making process. Old tales focus on the healing properties of this precious commodity, with butter made in the month of May thought to have special healing powers. As a result, the rural housewife would keep a small piece of 'May butter', then mix it with herbs to soothe scalds and burns at a later date. Each county had its own ideas and Lincolnshire legend would have us believe that throwing salt into the fire before churning would guarantee a good batch of butter. Lancashire tales spoke of putting a hot iron into the cream during the process to expel the witch from the churn, whilst a Gaelic superstition required sods of turf, or cinders to be laid beneath the churn to stop the fairies from stealing the butter.

In Ireland, some believed that if a visitor arrived at the house whilst the churning was taking place, then he was expected to take a turn. If he refused, he was called a 'Balor', after 'Balor of the Evil Eye', king of the giants and a legendary figure in Irish mythology, whose eye was said to have remained open once slain, its deadly beam burning a hole into the earth. Being given this title would apparently bring bad luck, so the cream would have to be removed from the churn.

To complete the butter-making process, 'butter pats' were made with ridged wooden paddles known as 'Scotch Hands', used to stabilise the butter into one-pound blocks and shape them ready for storage or sale. Some blocks were wrapped in printed paper, but wooden stamps made of sycamore – a wood that did not taint the flavour of the butter – also gave the option of impressing a pattern into the pats to identify the maker. Designs on stamps could include thistles, crowns, cows and swans.

Fluctuating food prices became a regular topic in the periodicals of the day. A column in *The Penny Magazine* of 1835 refers to the soaring cost of butter in different parts of the country:

With respect to the prices of butter, it appears by the household book of Lord North that a pound of butter in the reign of Queen Elizabeth cost four pence: at the present time, a pound of best butter in the West of England costs from seven pence to eight pence, while in the metropolis the price is fourteen pence.

A Hedgerow Harvest

Like their urban cousins, plenty of rural labourers had very little to eat. Poverty was not limited to the industrial cities, and country folk on limited means could find life equally tough. Food that was affordable and provided basic nutrition, tended to be starchy and pulse-based, with porridge, gruel and sago pudding top of the menu. When we think of gruel, the fictional character of Oliver Twist immediately springs to mind, as he summons up the courage to confront the workhouse overseer and, holding out his bowl he asks, 'Please, sir, I want some more'. In the novel, Charles Dickens describes Oliver's diet of 'three meals of thin gruel a day, with an onion twice a week and half a roll on Sunday'.

Made of oats and flour boiled in water or milk to form a thin porridge or watery soup, gruel was not only eaten by the poor, but was also part of the daily diet of some middle-class families. Emily Brontë mentions this in *Wuthering Heights* – 'but you've caught cold: I saw you shivering, and you must have some gruel to drive it out', the housekeeper Mrs Dean comments, as she bustles off to fetch Lockwood a warming dish. Similarly, in Jane Austen's *Emma* Mr Woodhouse enjoys eating gruel to restore his health. This dish may have consisted of very few ingredients and lacked flavour without the addition of salt, but it was considered the perfect meal to maintain strength and energy.

Country housewives became clever at making ends meet, supplementing meagre supplies and duller dishes with whatever 'free food' they could acquire. Even the children had a part to play and they were sent out mushrooming in the fields, to gather beech and cobnuts in season, berries from the hedgerows, fallen crab apples from the woodland and watercress from the streams. At the end of the harvest they would 'glean' the fields for vegetables which had been overlooked, collect wild garlic and herbs to flavour soups and stews, or catch pigeons to make a hearty pigeon pie.

To avoid spending the little money they had, country-people used a barter system with their neighbours, swapping produce, or an item they already had a quantity of, for another ingredient that they required. Those with a large patch of rhubarb might swap a few sticks with a neighbour who had a glut of beans, whilst those with extra hen's eggs might trade them for a bag of flour.

Those living on the edge of a country estate might even risk a spot of poaching – catching fish from the rivers and bagging the odd pheasant or rabbit for their table. Seen as a nuisance because they could entirely destroy a crop of vegetables, and as a blessing providing meat for the table the wild rabbit was among the poacher's most sought-after quarry. Yet, catching them was by no means an easy task.

An 1852 newspaper cutting outlines a recipe and procedure to help make the a task little easier:

To take wild rabbits alive:
Approach the warren, or holes, very quietly and place a small purse net, the same as are used for ferreting, over the mouth of each hole, then put a common tobacco pipe full of the preparation hereafter named, into the mouth of each hole, always on the windward side of the warren only, and ignite it with a Lucifer match. After igniting, close up the opening.

The preparation is made thus: Dissolve two drachms of Nitrate of Potash in one ounce of water, then wet one ounce of tobacco with the solution, freely sprinkling it with half a drachm of Cayenne Pepper. Let it dry gradually in the sun, or by a very slow fire, and it will be ready for use.

To make rabbits bolt for shooting:
Put the same preparation in the opening of the holes, on the windward side, stand perfectly still in a convenient place and shoot the rabbits as they leave their holes.

[NB: A *drachm* was a unit of weight formerly used by apothecaries and equivalent to 60 grains or one eighth of an ounce. Lucifer matches were a brand marketed by Samuel Jones and known for their bad burning odour; they even carried a warning that people with delicate lungs should not use them.]

Medicinal Remedies in the Victorian Kitchen

Early Victorian country recipe books tended to focus on remedies, rather than instructions of how to prepare a certain dish, as the lack of ingredients meant that most housewives knew their limited repertoire off by heart. Instead, it was customary to take clippings of interest from newspapers and other publications and paste them into a scrapbook or jot them down in a journal. Illness and infirmity of both livestock and family members was always a concern and, with little or no funds to pay for medical practitioners, any remedies were duly noted and treated seriously.

In 1882, the Byram family cut out the following cure for smallpox or scarlet fever from *The Weekly Post*, which relied on the powerful plant foxglove. There is no evidence to suggest that they ever had cause to try it out, though.

> Sulphate of Zinc – one grain
> Foxglove (Digitalis) – one grain
> One half teaspoon of sugar

Mix with two tablespoonfuls of water, when the above has been thoroughly mixed, add another 4 oz of water. Take one teaspoon every hour ... the disease will disappear in 12 hours ... for a child - smaller doses according to age.

Not all nineteenth century recipes were concerned with curing such severe diseases, but instead used natural remedies to help ease ailments suffered on a daily basis, treating them with herbs and plants collected from the kitchen garden. The humble stinging nettle was particularly highly esteemed by our ancestors. 'Nettle tea, made by boiling six handfuls of washed nettles in a quart of water, is one of the best blood purifiers', reported one Victorian newspaper's 'Health from Field and Garden' column, also claiming that 'People liable to spots and other skin eruptions drink it in large quantities'. Chickweed was declared to be 'one of nature's best remedies for skin troubles and should be well washed in salt water, then boiled like spinach, for which it makes a cheap and appetising substitute'.

Wood Sorrell, 'with its brilliant green leaves and pink stem', was seen as another valuable salad plant and again said to be 'largely used in France as a tonic and blood purifier'. No matter how hard life was for the cottager, it seems that taking care of the skin and restoring vigour in both the young and the old by cleansing the body of impurities was just as important, at least according to the newspaper.

Further advice from the same column states that bilious attacks could be alleviated by 'pouring boiling water over a handful of sage leaves, a cut up lemon and half an ounce of sugar' and this was believed to be 'splendid for digestion ... relieving pain and also improving the condition of the stomach and digestive organs generally'.

The medicinal properties of vegetables too, were highly recommended:

Onions are amongst the finest nervines known, and a splendid sedative. A large boiled onion, taken before going to bed, would ensure a good restful sleep and soothe the entire nervous system ... The milky juice of a lettuce, too, possesses valuable sedative properties and is most useful for calming jaded nerves and calming the mind to sleep.

Chapter Four

Preserving Produce

*A thriving household depends on the use of seasonal produce and the
application of common sense.*

(Olivier de Serres, *Theatre d'Agriculture*, 1600)

In the majority of Victorian households the kitchen was a chiefly
female domain. Culinary tasks and chores were presided over by
the women and, in order to manage the family food budget, they were
responsible for stretching the summer produce to increase meagre
portions in the winter months. Consequently, preserving and pickling
techniques were passed down from mother to daughter.

Jam was first recorded as a kitchen cupboard ingredient during the
1730s. At this time sugar was expensive and because fruit jams required
large amounts of sugar to enable them to set, they were considered
a luxury. When sugar became more affordable and accessible to the
masses, jam production became less of an extravagance and merely a
way of extending the life of the produce. Whenever there was a glut of
summer fruits, jam-making ensured that the excess yield would give
the family diet a sugar boost and livened up even the stalest piece of
bread. The overall process was simple and only required a large pan in
which to boil up the fruit, along with the same weight in sugar.

Pectin is a carbohydrate which helps fruit jams to set. Currants,
gooseberries and plums naturally contain plenty of pectin, but soft
fruits such as strawberries can be lacking and require the help of a
little added lemon juice to draw out whatever pectin there is within
the fruit to aid the process. To test the consistency of the jam, a small
spoonful was placed on a saucer and, once cooled, the cook would run
her little finger through the jam to gauge the firmness of the set. A
slight wrinkled skin on top of the preserve confirmed that it was ready
for bottling.

Clear jams, often known as 'jellies', were made by removing the pips,
skin and other larger fruit particles. This could be done by softening
the fruit and then mashing it, before straining the pulp through a sieve,
or overnight through a piece of muslin, and then boiling this clear
strained juice with sugar to a setting point. It was essential to use non-

metallic utensils, such as a wooden spoon and glass jars for storage, as the metals could react with the acids in the fruit to give an unpleasant taste to the finished product. The jars would be sterilised in hot water and dried completely before bottling began, to ensure the jam would have a long shelf life.

Making marmalade was a much more time consuming task. The word 'marmalade' is thought to have first appeared in the English language in 1480 and, when citrus fruits grew more plentiful in Britain during the seventeenth century, it wasn't long before this fruity preserve became an essential item on the ordinary British breakfast table. When the marmalade cutter was developed in the mid 1800s, the metal device with its wooden handle could be screwed to the kitchen table, allowing the fruits and rind to be cut quickly and caught in a bowl placed beneath. Cast iron examples can be seen in the kitchens of Penrhyn Castle in North Wales and at Buckfast Abbey in Devon, but they soon became a vital piece of the cook's arsenal in many homes around the country.

Although the basic method was the same, everyone had their own tips and techniques to make the perfect batch of jam, jelly or marmalade. In the 'Useful Hints' section of an 1888 edition of the periodical *Leisure Hour*, one correspondent felt the need to write in with her own advice for readers:

For many years my jams never kept well; they either fermented or turned mouldy. My cooks in turn blamed the fruit, the place they were stored in, the sugar, but did not for a moment imagine they could be in fault. The secret is never to leave the preserving pan for one moment from the commencement of the proceedings, and not to skim the fruit.

I put as a rule one pound of sugar to each pound of fruit, and stir the mass well from the time it is put on the fire; as the scum rises, and when boiling has begun, I stir more vigorously. After a time the scum begins to boil itself clear. When quite clear, the jam thickens, and I then take the pan off the fire and put the jam into warmed jars. All the jams I have made this way are bright and clear, and some of the fruit has been gathered on a damp day. I find fifty minutes or an hour ample time for preserving ten pounds of fruit; allowing twenty minutes of brisk boiling. I have adopted this plan with an oil stove as well as an open fire and by this method waste of any kind is avoided.

An 1864 recipe for Damson and Apple Jam

1 kg damsons
1.25 kg cooking apples
1 kg sugar
100ml water

Stew the damsons in water for approximately 3 hours. Pour the juice into a preserving pan. Peel, core and quarter the apples, add to the damson juice and boil together for 30 minutes, stirring well. Add the sugar and stir until dissolved, then boil for 10 min. This gives a fine, smooth preserve.

Growing up in the late 1880s in a rural hamlet, Flora Thompson observed a soon to be lost way of life. Self-sufficiency in the countryside was essential and Flora discovered how to make the most of what ingredients were available, in particular the 'free foods' Mother Nature had to offer:

> Sloes and blackberries and elderberries could be picked from the hedgerows, dandelions and colts foot and cowslips from the fields, and the garden provided rhubarb, currants, gooseberries and parsnips. Jam was made from garden and hedgerow fruit … over an open fire and needed great care in the making.
>
> Some notable housewives made jelly. Crab apple trees abounded in the hedgerows and the children knew just where to go for red crabs, red and yellow streaked crabs, or crabs which hung like ropes of green onions on the branches. It seemed … a miracle when a basket of these, with nothing but sugar and water added, turned into jelly as clear and bright as a ruby.

The Darwin Cookbook

Born in Staffordshire in 1808, Emma Wedgwood Darwin became the wife of eminent naturalist and scientist, Charles Darwin. Throughout her life she managed to complete 60 diaries recording events, dinners with friends, the health of her family and the running of her household. Although many of the entries were simple observations, her comments and the diaries themselves give us a glimpse into this era. The most fascinating book that Emma created is her 1839 recipe book. With seven children, twelve servants and a husband to feed, she collected suitable recipes to use for various occasions, although it is not known whether Emma did any of the cooking herself. Charles also got involved, adding instructions on how to boil rice.

From pigeon pie and fillet of veal, to guidance notes on stewing pears and how to salt bacon and hams, Emma's recipes are concise and easy to follow. 'Stewing Vegetables the Mrs Collins Way' involved a lengthy cooking time and, one imagines, very little nutrients were left by the end, as she advises, 'Stew the vegetables for 2 hours in a little water, put broth to it and boil it up and put two eggs beat up with a little cream, flour and water. Season it and don't boil any more'.

Along with complete dishes, Emma put great importance on using and preserving fruit. One recipe for 'Lemon Pickle' had a kick of horseradish, but required stirring every day for two weeks. She includes advice on making raspberry jam, quince marmalade and preserving oranges whole and, should you have an excess of fruit, she suggests desserts like gooseberry cream and a very simple recipe that you can imagine her children thoroughly enjoying.

Emma Darwin's Apple Jelly

Take 1lb Apples, ½ lb Sugar Loaf, ½ pint Water.

Put the sugar and water to boil and a little lemon peel. Then put the apples to boil for two hours or more. Put it in a mould to cool and put some whipped cream over it.

Just like modern cookbooks, Emma's diaries have useful printed guides placed in the opening pages. One in particular is a chart of weights and measures. Many of the terms are no longer in common use, but in the 1800s, all would have been the essential units referred to by cooks and housekeepers to gauge the quantities of products in their larders, pantries and store cupboards. Known as the 'Table of Miscellaneous Articles', an example of each term has its converted quantity in 'lbs' written alongside.

A firkin of butter	56 lbs
A peck of salt	14 lbs
A bushel of salt	56 lbs
A chest of tea	84 lbs
A hogshead of pilchards	40 gallons
A tun of seed oil	236 gallons
A stone of cheese	16 lbs

Smoking and Salt Curing

As we have already learned, vinegar was a Victorian store cupboard favourite, invaluable for pickling vegetables, eggs and other mixtures of ingredients. But it was equally important to find ways to lengthen the life of any meat and fish acquired. If the family pig had been sent to slaughter, they would want to keep some of that meat to eat at a later date. The same would apply with poultry or fish, either caught locally, bought or traded.

One method of preservation would have been to set up a home smoking facility. This could be constructed simply through reusing an old barrel, tea chest, or any wooden box they could lay their hands on, big enough to hold the food to be preserved and with enough space around it to allow the smoke to freely circulate. Wooden sticks were suspended within, enabling the food to be hung from this makeshift apparatus. The whole contraption – which would also have had a large hole in the bottom – would be mounted upon stones and bricks to provide an area underneath, and towards the front, to add fuel. This was then lit and the smoke was naturally drawn up inside, smoking the food within.

The taste of the preserved meat, fish or game would depend upon the type of wood shavings and sawdust used as fuel. Oak and fruit woods would give a mellow flavour, which could be enhanced by adding any herb twigs from the cottage garden. Coal was never used as a fuel for smoke preservation techniques, as the resulting flavour was not pleasant.

Curing was a way of preserving meat, or fish such as cod or herring, using dry salt or a mixture of salt in water, known as brine. The salt acted as a way of drawing the liquid from the food item, making it less prone to bacterial infection and deterioration, and easier to store for longer periods of time.

The Benefits of Beekeeping

Britons have enjoyed honey since medieval times when religious communities kept bees for their wax, which was used to create superior candles to those made of tallow used by the majority of the population. Honey was found to be a natural sweetener long before cane and beet were processed into sugar. Once mixed with water and allowed to ferment, it could also be used to make delicious mead, which helped the monks to survive the long, cold winters.

Originally, honey was collected from the nests of wild bees, which were often located in the trunks of hollow trees. However, as people began to realise the benefits of this amber nectar, small straw hives known as 'skeps' were built, which encouraged the bees to create colonies, and also enabled the keepers to manage the honey production. A cone-shaped cover, known as a 'hackle', was added in bad weather to deflect the rain, and extra space could be created for the growing colony by attaching an additional chamber called an 'eke'. These two unusual words coined the phrases 'raising your hackles' and 'to eke something out', meaning to spread out.

Although for most country folk, beekeeping was not classed as an occupation, many of our rural ancestors kept a hive, or series of hives, adding honey to their food supplies. The goods produced from the fruits of the bees' labour could be eaten, used by the family or traded with neighbours and villagers for other surplus items. The home apiarist or beekeeper's job was to manage the bees, ensure they were well-fed, and to protect the colony from disease until their honey production was complete. This task could be carried out by both men and women and the skills involved were often passed down within the family.

Whilst rural cottagers found a sheltered area or recess near their property to house their coiled straw skeps, some stately homes chose to have purpose built bee houses. At Attingham Park in Shropshire, the bee house – located close to the walled garden – has now become a rare listed building. Dating from about 1805, and in use throughout the Victorian era, this elegant wooden construction comprises a lattice design which allowed the bees to travel freely to and from the straw skeps inside. A slate roof protected the hives – and the honey inside - from the elements.

By the late nineteenth century, the moveable hive had been invented, consisting of a series of wooden frames, where the bees could create a wax honey comb. Beeswax is secreted from special glands on their abdomens, then used to build the 'comb' – a series of six-sided cells strong enough to support the honey, store pollen and even rear their young. It is thought that a honey bee must eat between 15-20lbs of honey to produce each pound of beeswax.

Victorian cooks experimented with ways of using honey as a natural sweetener within their dishes. They mixed it with mustard or the zest of an orange, to create glazes for meat dishes; combined it with butter and a teaspoon of rum to make a delicious paste to spread on fruit loaves, tea breads, scones and toast; and enlivened the taste and texture of a variety of cakes and puddings with one or two spoonfuls.

Sometimes, the smallest amount of honey could help provide the flavour that a cook was seeking to complete a recipe. In his 1849 cookbook, *The Modern Housewife*, Alexis Soyer gave the instructions on how to create his version of 'Cooling Lemonade':

> Put a quart of water in a stew pan to boil, into which put two moist dried figs, each split in two; let it boil a quarter of an hour, then have ready the peel of a lemon, taken off rather thickly, and the half of the lemon cut in thin slices; throw them into the stew pan, and boil two minutes longer; pour it into the jug, which cover closely with paper until cold, then pass it through a sieve: add a teaspoon of honey and it is ready for use.

As honey dissolved extremely easily, it was a natural choice for use in a number of flavoured beverages. English journalist and author Robert Kemp Philip chose to use honey as one of the main ingredients when he devised a recipe for Apple Wine in his *Dictionary of Daily Wants*, published in 1859. It required the reader to:

> Braise two bushels of apples, and put them in a gallon and a half of cold water; add seven pounds of honey, three pints of rum, one ounce of white tartar, and a nutmeg grated; boil it as long as any scum arises, then strain it through a sieve, and let it cool; add some good yeast, and stir it well; let it work in a tub for two or three weeks, then skim off the head, draw the liquor clear off, and turn it.

For those tasked with collecting the honey, it was originally thought that certain types of perfume and odours annoyed the bees and encouraged them to sting. The Romans believed that the bees should not be tended to if the keeper had not washed, had recently drunk alcohol or eaten strongly flavoured food. Charles Butler, regarded as the 'Father of English Beekeeping' and author of *The Feminine Monarchie* (1609), thought that as long as you washed your face and hands in a malt liquor and approached the bees carrying a bunch of sweetly-smelling herbs, there would be no need for protective clothing to shield you from their stings.

But many beekeepers did feel the need for some sort of safeguard. During the Victorian era a variety of outfits were worn, ranging from wooden masks to leather or oiled linen gloves with gauntlets. A hood with a drawstring around the neck was used to shield the face, a blouse-like top with ties at the sleeves and a fully-enclosed suit were just some of the designs that developed with the changing fashions. Broad-brimmed hats, one of the less fantastic beekeeping contraptions, were in use in England as early as 1200, and over the centuries the addition of a fine mesh veil ensured maximum protection for the face and neck.

Portable smokers were carried, enabling the keeper to aim a blast of smoke into the hive to 'subdue' the bees for a short time and allow him to remove any honey combs, inspect the hives and carry out minor repairs, lessening his chances of getting stung. Honey extractors became popular from the 1860s onwards, enabling the frames of honeycomb to be placed inside a box-like device, which was then rotated using a hand crank to spin the honey from the comb ready for bottling.

A traditional beekeeper writing under the pseudonym of 'Bee Orchis' in an 1890 edition of *The Girl's Own Paper*, explained that investing in your own apiary wasn't always plain sailing:

> One summer I bought another swarm off a neighbour, but it was a continual trouble to me, as the bees proved so savage a disposition that it was difficult to do anything with them. I gave 10 shillings for them, and after they had yielded me a little over 10 shillings worth of honey, the other bees invaded the hive, killed the rightful owners, and cleared out every morsel of their stores. I believe that they must have lost their Queen which had taken away the desire to defend themselves. Thankfully, I now have ten colonies hard at work producing honey.

Most country beekeepers were so in tune with their swarm that they felt able to wear only relatively little protection when tending them. Others, had a particular outfit that they donned for the task at hand, and 'Bee Orchis' recommended similar apparel for anyone new to the practicalities of beekeeping.

> My 'bee dress' consists of a broad brimmed hat, with a deep, round veil of green blind-muslin, which is carefully tucked into the collar of

an old, light-coloured Ulster with no folds in which a bee can lodge, and a pair of bee-gloves - two thick cotton pairs, one over the other. Some people recommend you to work with these gloves wet. Long cuffs are attached to these to draw up over the sleeves, gathered in with an elastic. Initially, I adopted a pair of old cloth riding trousers, with the strap under the foot, which I found to be a great protection from an angry bee which has the unpleasant habit of crawling under your raiment and inflicting a sting when you least expect it.

Keeping the bees happy and content was vital, as we have discovered. It has been known for the introduction of a new hive to be invaded by the bees from neighbouring hives; the intruders stealing the stores of honey and killing the rightful owners. If the queen bee is killed, the worker bees may lack the desire to defend themselves and abandon the hive altogether. Honey was a precious commodity, so it was equally important to ensure the new hives were scrubbed clean before a swarm was introduced, to safeguard against diseases that could decimate a colony.

Each beekeeper also had their own recipes for supplementing the bees' diets and keeping them well-fed. Some added a bottle of syrup to the frame of the hive, made using half a pint of water to a pound of sugar, with the addition of a few drops of salicylic acid solution. Others boiled 6lbs of loaf sugar with ½pt of water to make a solid mass, to ensure that the bees would not starve over the long winter months. In spring, this candy was made by adding a pound of pea, or wheat flour, to the mix as a substitute for the yellow dust or pollen, which the bees gathered from the flowers, helping to feed the next generation within the hive.

Not only the honey was beneficial to the beekeeper's family. It was said to take the bees as long to make 1lb of wax as it did to make 20lbs of honey, so by saving each little morsel, rendering it down and straining it through a course oiled flannel into an oiled basin, could increase the household income by about 1s 6d per pound if sold on to a chemist's or oil shop.

Family journals provide us with an insight into just how important the 'honey harvest' was to Victorian beekeepers. An early nineteenth century recipe, taken from handwritten notes in 'Mr Shuttleworth's Gardening Book', explains that 'the best honey should be used to make good mead'. A long process of fermentation, preparation and bottling is then required, but a tip is given to guide home cooks to recognise what the lethal brew should look like: 'With respect to strength, the honey should be mixed with somewhat more than its weight in water – soft, fine water is best. Boil till much of the water is evaporated, that the liquor will float an egg on its surface without it sinking much more than half its diameter'.

Whilst Mr Shuttleworth took pains to underline the importance of using only the best honey, the Wright family of Bollington – whose mid-Victorian recipes and correspondence is preserved in the Cheshire Archives and Local Studies Library – were more concerned with keeping notes on the medicinal benefits of the substance. They used some of their honey in an early form of cough mixture, the recipe requiring 'a tablespoonful of honey, the same of oatmeal, a lump of butter about the size of a egg and a pint of boiling water, stir it well all the while you pour the water on. Take this instead of your supper until your cough is well'.

Curious Beekeeping Customs

Considered extremely important to community life from mediaeval times right up to the latter part of the nineteenth century, bees were revered not only for the production of their honey but also for their rumoured 'mystical' powers. Stories and superstition were passed down through the generations, with many believing that the bees had a special knowledge of the future.

Consequently, the bees were informed of all family details, especially marriages, births and deaths – failure to do so could result in the swarm leaving the hive. Even after a wedding it was customary to leave a piece of cake by the hive. Such was their rumoured sensitivity, that folklore dictated that if a girl could walk through a swarm without being stung she could be declared a virgin, whilst those young women who were stung must be of dubious character.

Even the flight of the bees was thought to indicate mixed omens, foretelling good harvests such as in the following rhyme:

> *A swarm of bees in May, is worth a load of hay,*
> *And a swarm of bees in July, is hardly worth the fly.*

A swarm settling on the roof of a property also predicted an imminent death in the family, yet a lone bee buzzing inside the house was said to signify the arrival of a visitor.

Chapter Five

Regional & Seasonal Cuisine

Religion feeds the soul, Education the mind, Food the body.
(Alexis Soyer, *The Pantropheon or A history of food and its
preparation in ancient times*, 1853)

By the nineteenth century, Britain had already developed regional
dishes featuring produce more accessible in or specific to certain
areas. Rural and coastal communities in particular, developed their own
recipes based on the ingredients they could easily lay their hands upon,
which were also strongly determined by the seasons. While the wealthy
had access to a much wider range of food products, the working classes
had to sustain their families and come up with appetising meals from a
much simpler variety of ingredients.

As an island, Britain has always had a ready supply of seafood,
although fish has been in and out of favour on aristocratic dining tables.
In 1845 Eliza Acton's *Modern Cookery for Private Families* warned that
'nothing can more effectually destroy the appetite, or disgrace the cook,
than fish sent to table imperfectly cleaned. Handle it lightly, and never
throw it roughly about, so as to bruise it'.

Since the medieval period, on Fridays and during Lent the church
had imposed restrictions on the consumption of meat, ensuring that
on these occasions it was set aside in favour of the gifts of the sea. By
the nineteenth century, fleets of oyster smacks were making a living
dredging the Sussex coast, resulting in a glut of seafood becoming
cheaply available to the masses. Stalls at London's Billingsgate Market
could be seen piled high with mountains of the grey shelled delicacies.
Costermongers stacked their handcarts with them, peddling oysters
around the streets, selling them for up to four pence a dozen and serving
them with salt, pepper and vinegar. Whelks were equally popular along
with soused or pickled, herrings.

Charles Dickens made a reference to the excess of oysters in the
capital in his 1836 novel, *The Pickwick Papers*: 'The poorer a place is
the greater call there seems for oysters. Look here, Sir, here's an oyster
stall to every half dozen houses - the street's lined with 'em. Blessed if

I don't think that when a man's very poor, he rushes out of his lodgings and eats oysters in regular desperation'. The trend continued until the beds were overfished and only the wealthy could afford to serve oysters on their dinner tables.

Writers and novelists have always been quick to pick up on cultural changes and their observations on the Victorian culinary world give us an indication as to what was in or out of favour at any particular time. Food fashions created greater demand, so when turtle meat was imported to Britain from the Orient, Green Turtle Soup became all the rage. But the cost of the ingredients required meant that this particular dish was only affordable to those at the more affluent end of society. Not to be outdone, less well-off aspiring gourmands concocted an alternative version, the aptly named 'Mock Turtle Soup', using the non-muscular meat from the hooves, head and tail of a calf to replicate the texture of the turtle meat.

Such was its popularity that it even got a mention in Lewis Carroll's 1865 novel *Alice's Adventures in Wonderland:*

> "Have you seen the Mock Turtle yet?"
> "No," said Alice. "I don't even know what a Mock Turtle is."
> "It's the thing a Mock Turtle Soup is made from," said the Queen.

Scottish Sustenance

During the first half of the nineteenth century, it was traditional for those 'north of the border' to start the day with a bowl of oatmeal porridge made with milk. Writing for *The Girl's Own Paper* in 1882, cook Mary Brechin gives us a wider insight into the Scottish diet and explains how those with a little more money to spare would enjoy the Sunday treat of a 'tea breakfast':

> This would consist of tea, bannocks, scones, home cured pork and eggs; and, in places near the coast, of fresh herring, haddocks, or cod. This 'tea breakfast' was only partaken of by the older people, the bairns getting their porridge as usual. The only occasion on which this rule was broken being New Year's morning, when the youngsters were allowed to eat as much as they could of good things.

In the mid-1800s, loaf breads were a fairly recent addition to the Scottish menu. Traditionally, households baked scones, oatmeal cakes and bannocks upon a flat piece of iron about a half-inch thick, known as a griddle. A bow handle was attached to the griddle, so that it could be lifted above the fire for cooking.

For the Scottish labouring classes, dinner – taken around midday – usually consisted of broth, served with boiled potatoes. Dessert was just a handful of berries plucked from the hedgerows. Even then, this fruit was too highly prized to be eaten regularly in this way and would instead have been collected and made into jellies and jams for the household. Blackcurrants were especially sought after, not only for the table, but also for the traditional belief in the curative properties of the berries for coughs and colds. Supper took place when the men returned home in the evening. Brose, an uncooked form of porridge consisting of oatmeal mixed with boiling water and eaten with salt, butter, milk or cheese, made a regular appearance on the labourer's supper table.

The middle classes enjoyed a broth, perhaps followed by stewed mutton and haggis, washed down with tea or beer. As Mary Brechin notes:

> Perhaps the most striking point in Scotch as compared with English cookery is the difference between the broth of the one nation and the soup of the other. While the English put the meat, bones, and vegetables into a stock pot, simmer until most of the goodness is extracted, and then strain; the Scotch put all the ingredients into a broth pot, simmer until thoroughly cooked, take out the meat, which is eaten with potatoes, and serve the broth just as it is, without any further preparation, thus producing a dish quite as nourishing and far more satisfying than that of their English neighbours.
>
> Scotch broth is often prepared without any meat at all, dripping being used instead. The vegetables sliced, barley, pepper, and salt added, and, when nearly ready, a few potatoes are put in and boiled along with the broth until nicely, but not too much, cooked. Potatoes are often added to what is called 'second day's broth' – that is, broth left over from the previous day's dinner and reheated – when the potatoes used may be either uncooked or cooked, although the latter are preferable as their flavour is much finer.

Throughout the seventeenth, eighteenth and nineteenth centuries, working-class Scottish families had to make use of every little scrap of food they came by. Money was tight, and poor harvests and lack of produce made each meal a real challenge. The demands of feeding large families and hard-labouring menfolk dictated that the woman of the house had to be extremely inventive with relatively few ingredients. One of the most notable aspects of the Scottish diet is the amount of offal consumed, as thrifty cooks made the most of every carcass.

Some of Mary Brechin's recipes were not for the faint-hearted. Although these traditional 1880s-style Scottish recipes would have provided nourishment for the whole family, it is unlikely that many housewives today would attempt the preparation and cooking of the 'delicacies' below.

Sheep's Head Broth

Get a good sheep's head, singe it, cut the eyes, and thoroughly rub the head with the liquid, and soak in salt and water for a night. In the morning thoroughly clean the head, and soak in salted water for an hour. Put the head into a saucepan with pepper, salt, and three gallons of water; skin well, and boil for three hours. Take out the head, and put half a teaspoon of well washed barley, a Savoy (cabbage), carrot, turnip and four leeks, nicely sliced, into the stock; simmer for about three hours longer, and serve.

Once this gruesome preparation and initial cooking was complete, you not only had a tasty broth to serve but also a whole, meaty sheep's head to create other meals with. The unappetising jelly created by boiling the head along with calf's feet, straining the liquid and clarifying the jelly with a little calf brain, was considered a nourishing dish for invalids. Alternatively, a sheep's head made a filling pie or potted meat:

Sheep's Head Pie

Take half of the head which was boiled for broth, cut into nice pieces, using all the skin; season nicely with the ground cloves, Jamaica (now known as allspice), black, and white pepper, salt, a little parsley, and a hard-boiled egg, if liked. Put into a pie dish that will just hold it. Cut the tongue into neat slices, and arrange them on the top. Moisten the whole with a little stock; cover with a nice short crust, and bake about one hour.

Potted Head

Take the other half of the head, chopping very small, and put into a saucepan with sufficient stock to just cover it; season with Jamaica, black, and white pepper, and salt; simmer slowly for three hours, and pour into a mould. When going to serve it, loosen the edges, reverse the mould of a dish, when it will slip out quite easily. Garnish, and serve.

One of the most well-known uses for offal is in the Scottish national dish of haggis. Continuing her series of Scottish cookery articles, Mary Brechin provides advice on how to prepare your own haggis, including a tip for those who found the experience a little challenging:

Haggis

Procure a bag [sheep's stomach] from the butcher; soak in salt water for a night; next morning scrape it well, and wash in boiling water; rub it over with salt, and soak in water until required. Boil a sheep's draft or pluck [the heart, liver, windpipe and lungs of a slaughtered animal] for two hours; when cold, grate the liver, and heart and lights [the lungs] very finely, removing all pieces of vein and stringy parts; mix with this one pound of pork suet, minced very small, and two pounds of coarse oatmeal; season with salt and different kinds of pepper; mix well, using a little of the liquid that the 'pluck' was boiled in to moisten it with. Fill the bag, secure the mouth with a skewer, and plunge into boiling water; prick the bag with a fork to prevent it bursting, and boil for four hours.

Tip – Haggis may be made in a jar and thus save the trouble of cleaning the bag.

Cockles and Mussels: A Taste of Wales

Over the centuries, Wales's natural resources have provided employment for thousands and, as a result, Welsh food has developed to satisfy the appetites of hard-working farm labourers, coal miners and quarrymen.

Prior to modern food manufacture and processing techniques, our Welsh ancestors relied upon ingredients they had grown themselves, keeping animals to provide meat and dairy products, and foraging in the hedgerows, fields and rivers for food they could pick and gather without any monetary outlay. They were entirely dependent upon the seasons, and upon what Mother Nature could provide. As in the rest of the British Isles, Welsh families living near the coast had the widest variety of extra resources to bring to the table, as hundreds of fishing communities quietly made their livelihoods by selling their catch and using it to feed their families.

Mussels have been found in North Wales since prehistoric times, with the *Mya Margaritifera* variety, or in Welsh *Cragen y Diluw*, being most sought after, not just for their meat, but also as pearl producers. Legend has it that Welsh merchant, Sir Richard Wynne of Gwydir, presented the wife of Charles I, Queen Henrietta Maria, with a pearl found in a Conwy mussel. During the early 1800s, over four kilos of pearls were sent from the harbour town of Conwy to London jewellers every week, but collecting these prized jewels was no easy task. The musselling season ran between September and April, when the fishermen would wait for the tide and then head out in their boats to the mussel beds. The tools used were basic for such a hazardous job, requiring the men to use an 18ft rake to scrape the mussels off the beds and haul them onto their little boats. Pearl agents would deal with the local fishermen, weigh the pearls using small scales, agree a price and arrange transportation of the cargo to the capital.

The shellfish business also ensured work for the womenfolk, who would gather mussels from the shore or prize them from rocks, scraping them clean with a small knife fashioned with a spoon-shaped blade, binding their hands to protect them from the sharp shells. In the town they would help out in the pearling kitchens, where the mussels were 'mashed' to extract the tiny seed pearls and the remains recycled. Evidence of this old tradition, in the form of crushed mussel shells, has been found in the foundations of some of Conwy's oldest buildings.

Mussel meat was a rich source of protein, and could soon be made into a nutritious meal for the fishermen and their families. It was important to only prepare those still alive, as any that had perished before cooking could cause food poisoning. The shells were scraped and their wispy protruding beard was removed; any not firmly closed were discarded. The mussels would then be placed in a large pan with a very little liquid and steamed with the lid on until the shells opened and the meat was revealed. The wealthier classes also enjoyed this dish, cooking their mussels in wine.

Cockles were another staple food of the Welsh fisherman's table. Penclawdd on the Gower Peninsula was one of the most popular cockle-gathering areas. Originally a female task, the women of Penclawdd would work along the shoreline in all weathers, as they carried out the back-breaking job of extracting the shellfish from the beach. A short handled rake was used to draw the cockles out of the sand, before sieving them through a 'riddle' to ensure that the smaller cockles were left to increase in size and replenish the beds.

Their work was often hazardous, especially in foggy conditions which could distract the pickers, leaving them stranded on the sand and surrounded by the incoming tide. A good knowledge of the local geography was essential. Once collected, the harvest was transported from the beach on donkeys and sold throughout the villages.

The women developed a distinctive outfit, wearing multiple layers of clothing covered by a customary dress of red and black, which would be pinned up at the waist to reveal a Welsh flannel petticoat beneath. A shawl covered their shoulders and an apron protected their dress from the muddy sand. A smaller version of the Welsh hat, known as a cockle bonnet, was trimmed with white lace and topped with a thick pad called a 'doreb', which cushioned their heads and hats from the weight of the cockle pail or basket.

Back in the kitchen, the Welsh enjoyed their cockles cooked with lamb or as the filling in a pie, topped with shortcrust pastry, but traditionally cockles formed an accompaniment to laverbread. Still gathered today off the Gower Peninsula and the Pembrokeshire and Carmarthen coasts, laver is an edible form of seaweed, high in protein, iron and vitamins. It was the breakfast dish of eighteenth century pit workers, whilst by the mid-nineteenth century it was often made into a hot sauce and served with mutton. Over the years, laverbread (in Welsh, *bara lafwr* or *bara lawr*) has become a Welsh delicacy. Made by boiling the seaweed for several hours, mincing it into a paste and sprinkling it with oatmeal before frying, it is served with bacon and cockles as part of a traditional Welsh breakfast.

Primarily a food source, seaweed was also gathered to be dried and burnt as fuel, then either dug into the land or burned and the ashes sprinkled over the soil to act as manure. Men and women raked the seaweed from the shoreline before their harvest was collected off the beaches by horse and cart and spread out in drying huts.

Barmbrack and Boxty: The Irish Influence

The humble potato had a devastating effect on the population of Ireland during the 1840s blight, but it was also to influence the country's cuisine. Many of Ireland's national dishes rely on potato, including: Irish Stew, known as *Stobhach Gaelach*, made from mutton, potatoes, onion and parsley; Colcannon, a hearty, yet simple combination of potatoes, kale, scallions, milk and butter; and Boxty, potato pancake made from finely grated raw potato and mashed potato, mixed with flour, baking soda and buttermilk.

Such was the popularity of these potato-based dishes, that the methods and memories of creating these meals even inspired folk songs:

Did you ever eat Colcannon, made from lovely pickled cream?
With the greens and scallions mingled like a picture in a dream.
Did you ever make a hole on top to hold the melting flake
Of the creamy, flavoured butter that your mother used to make?

They also warned of the possible consequences if you didn't make the dish properly:

Boxty on the griddle,
Boxty on the pan,
If you can't bake boxty
Sure you'll never get a man.

As in the rest of the British Isles, in Ireland bread formed a large part of the working class diet. The Irish often preferred soda bread, a quick alternative to yeast-baked bread, made using wheat flour, sodium bicarbonate, salt, and buttermilk, to create a filling loaf, or farl (the traditional name for a flat piece of triangular-shaped bread). Barmbrack, a yeasted bread with the addition of raisins and sultanas, was baked as part of Irish Halloween customs. Into the mix, a pea, a stick, a piece of cloth, a small coin (originally a silver sixpence) and a ring were added.

Once cooked, each item acted as a fortune-telling device when received in a slice of the sweet-smelling loaf. Whilst the ring foretold that the recipient would marry within the year, the pea signalled that its beneficiary would remain single; the stick meant an unhappy marriage or continual disputes; the cloth warned of bad luck or poverty, whereas whoever received the coin would enjoy good fortune.

A Calendar of Time-Honoured Traditions

Food still dominates our lives and many traditional religious holidays and festivals throughout the year focus upon it. During the Victorian era, families looked forward to these annual highlights and went out of their way to give thanks and observe related culinary customs.

Mothering Sunday
Also known as Mother's Day, this takes place on the fourth Sunday of Lent, the 40-day period leading up to Easter. Some believe that the celebrations were established to honour Cybele, the Roman Mother

Goddess. In Western Christianity, Mothering Sunday also became known as 'Refreshment Sunday' (or *Laetare* Sunday – the fourth Sunday of Lent), as the fasting rules which applied at this time were relaxed especially for this day.

Other origins can be linked to the early English term used by villagers of calling their nearest parish church, the 'Daughter Church'. By the seventeenth century, most children over the age of 10 were expected to seek work and contribute to the family income. They took positions as domestic servants, or apprenticeships to learn a trade. It was considered important that these children could travel back home once a year, so in the middle of Lent they were granted leave by their employers to return to the family home, and visit the 'Mother Church', or main parish church/cathedral in their area.

This holiday period became a time for reunions, festivities and family gatherings. The children would never return home empty-handed and brought gifts and bunches of flowers for their mothers to thank them for their hard work and love. Soon, it became traditional to bring a cake to celebrate the occasion. Known as a Simnel Cake, the name of this cake is thought to derive from the Latin word *simila*, a fine wheat flour used for cake-making. Numerous stories surround the origins of this custom; one proclaims that whilst making the cake, a couple named Simon and Nell could not decide whether the finished mixture should be baked or boiled, so they combined both cooking methods, and from then on, the Mothering Sunday cake was named in their honour – 'Sim – Nel'.

The cake itself was highly symbolic. It consisted of mixed fruit and was layered inside and on top with almond marzipan. The final embellishment comprised 11 balls of marzipan to represent Jesus's disciples. One disciple was purposefully left out to denote the betrayer Judas. Sometimes sugared violets or primroses completed the decoration.

Harvest Home

Harvest time has always been one of the most important dates on the British calendar. Its success or failure once dominated people's lives and the celebrations and traditions surrounding the event date back to Pagan times. To safeguard their harvest for the following year, Saxon farmers would offer the first cut sheaf of corn to their gods of fertility, whilst the last sheaf was thought to contain the 'Spirit of the Corn' and was accompanied by the sacrifice of an animal, usually a hare caught during the gathering of the crops. A model of the hare was then made from the corn to symbolise the continuity of the spirit and is thought to have been the forerunner to the art of creating 'corn dollies' or icons, hung within the farmhouse to represent the Goddess of the Grain. These figures would be kept until the following spring, when they would be ploughed back into the soil to ensure a successful crop in the year ahead.

Each year on 1 August, the period known as Lammas – from the Anglo-Saxon *hlaf-mas* or 'loaf mass' – was commemorated by the farmers who created loaves of bread made from the new crop of wheat to give to their local church. These loaves were then used during Holy Communion when a special mass was given, offering up a prayer to God in the hope of a successful harvest in the coming weeks. In some areas of England, it was also traditional for tenants to give freshly harvested wheat to their landlords.

Communities appointed a responsible man to become their 'Lord of the Harvest', and his role was to organise the field workers and negotiate their wages. When the crop gathering was complete, the last sheaves of corn were brought from the fields on a wagon and horses decorated with ribbons and garlands of flowers. The church bell was rung to allow the women and children to go gleaning, collecting any leftover crops they could find in the fields.

The Harvest Supper was laid on by farmers and landowners to reward their servants and workers for their weeks of hard graft, and the feast was eagerly anticipated by all those involved. At this time of year, Goose Fairs were also held in towns around the country to enable the farmers to sell the birds they had reared, which were now in their prime. The birds' feet were coated in a mixture of tar and sand to protect them on their journeys, as they were driven from the countryside to the town to be sold. As a result, a goose, roasted and stuffed with apples, was the perfect accompaniment to the freshly picked vegetables at the Harvest Supper.

The British tradition of celebrating Harvest Festival was transferred to the Church in 1843, instigated by the Rev Robert Hawker when he invited local parishioners to his church at Morwenstow in Cornwall for a special thanksgiving service. The custom of decorating the church with newly harvested produce and flowers, whilst singing Victorian hymns such as 'We Plough the Fields and Scatter' and 'All Things Bright and Beautiful' is centred around farming traditions. It is still enjoyed in communities today on the Sunday when the harvest full moon occurs closest to the autumn equinox in late September or early October.

Hallowmas

Hallowmas is the collective name for three celebrations which take place during the last day of October and the first few days of November, combining the Eve of All Saints, All Saints' Day and All Souls' Day. This period of commemoration developed from the Celtic festival of Samhain, when the Celts believed that evil spirits appeared as darkness fell. Bonfires were lit as a deterrent and parades took place, with villagers dressing up in costumes to represent saints, angels and devils.

Various food stuffs have played their part in the ancient rituals surrounding this event. When the Romans incorporated their own customs into British traditions they ensured that these festivities were also used to celebrate the previous harvest, honouring Pomona, their goddess of fruit and trees. Pomona's emblem was that of the apple, which may have eventually led to the fun practice of 'apple bobbing', where the superstitious believe that the first to bite into the fruit will be the first to marry the following year.

For the early Christians, All Hallows' Eve signalled a time when the souls of those departed were released from purgatory to walk the earth for 48 hours – a continuation of the old pagan belief that the spirits of the dead could directly affect those of the living on this particular night. Another superstition surrounding this night involved travellers, who were advised to carry a piece of bread crossed with salt to repel witches and ensure that their journey was completed before midnight.

Many of the traditions carried out at Hallowmas developed from ancient myths and legends. One Irish folktale tells of a miser named Jack who, because of his meanness could not enter heaven; neither could he enter hell, as he played tricks on the devil, so his punishment was to roam the earth for all time. To light his path he was given a piece of coal by the devil, which Jack placed in a turnip he had been eating. In memory of this event, and with the turnip and pumpkin both in abundance at this time of year, the Jack o' Lantern, or pumpkin lantern, was created, carved with the laughing face of Jack and hollowed out to place a lighted candle inside to keep the evil spirits at bay.

As All Hallows' Eve disappeared with the night, All Saints' Day arose with the morning sun and was celebrated annually on the 1 November. Primarily dedicated to feasting, the Anglicans and Roman Catholics took the opportunity to remember the long line of Christian saints and martyrs without a specific festival day of their own. They were expected to attend church for the occasion and not take part in any laborious work. While All Saints' Day paid tribute to those in heaven, All Souls' Day took place on the following day and was used to remember those who remained in the state of purgatory. By honouring and praying for those who had died, their souls would be purified and move on into Heaven, cleansed of all sin. Victorian children would parade through the village singing the rhyme:

> *Soul, Soul, a soul cake!*
> *I pray thee, good missus, a soul cake!*
> *One for Peter, two for Paul, three for Him what made us all!*

They would ask for food for the departed, which would later be donated to feed the hungry. The food given was often in the form of soul cakes and by exchanging a cake, prayers would be said for the donor's deceased relatives.

Soul Cake Recipe

3/4 lb. flour
6ox sugar
6oz butter
1 egg
1½ teaspoons vinegar
½ teaspoonful cinnamon,
½ teaspoonful mixed spice and a pinch nutmeg

First mix the dry ingredients together, rub in the fat and add the egg and vinegar. Knead the dough until soft, cut into rounds and bake for 20 minutes.

Wassailing

Associated with passing on good wishes to family and friends at Christmas and New Year, Wassailing originated from the Old English term *Waes hael*, meaning 'be well'. It was traditional for the Saxon lord of the manor to shout *waes hael* at the beginning of each year to his assembled villagers, who would reply *drinc hael*, meaning 'drink and be healthy'.

As time went on, people began travelling door-to-door during the Christmas season, bearing good wishes and a wassail bowl of an ale-based drink seasoned with spices and honey. The ingredients varied from county to county. Along the way they would sing the popular 'Wassailing Carol':

Here we come a wassailing
Among the leaves so green,
Here we come a wassailing,
So fair to be seen.
Love and joy come to you,
And to you your wassail too,
And God bless you and send you, A happy New Year,
And God send you,
A happy New Year.

Even the act of collecting the apples to make the wassail was surrounded by custom and tradition. The apple trees were sprinkled with wassail to ensure a good crop and the villagers would gather around them banging on pots and pans to make a tremendous noise and scare away any demons by waking the 'Sleeping Tree Spirit'. Cider was poured over the roots of the biggest tree and pieces of toast steeped in the liquor were placed within the branches. The wassail song was also sung to bless the apple harvest for the following year:

Apple Tree Wassail
Oh apple tree, we'll wassail thee,
And hoping thou wilt bear
For the Lord does know where we may go,
To be merry another year.

Although these old traditions are now being revived in some areas, they were especially important during a time when landlords needed a good apple crop to attract willing workers, as labourers were often paid in cider.

A Culinary Christmas

The Christmas pudding had seen many guises before establishing itself as part of our festive lunch. Originally, versions known as plum pottage or frumenty, were created using a mixture of mutton or beef in broth, thickened with raisins, currants and prunes, along with breadcrumbs, spices and wine. This was traditionally eaten as a first course. When Thomas Kibble Hervey wrote his *Book of Christmas* in 1836, he described the pudding forerunner as 'a spiced gruel sweetened with dried fruit', but over the years, the recipe changed when the mixture was thickened with eggs. Later, the meat was left out, but suet remained and the dish became a dessert.

Cassell's 1875 *Dictionary of Cookery* provides a fitting description of this culinary legacy:

> The plum pudding is a national dish, and is despised by foreign nations because they can never make it fit to eat. In almost every family there is a recipe for it, which has been handed down from mother to daughter through two or three generations, and which never has been and never will be equalled, much less surpassed, by any other ...
>
> If well made, Christmas plum pudding will be good for twelve months.

Steeped in religious tradition, even the making of the pudding required certain rituals. 'Stir Up Sunday' – practised on the first Sunday of Advent – was the correct date upon which to create the dessert, requiring the pudding makers to stir the mix in a circular motion from east to west, to symbolise the journey of the Magi. Many recipes included 13 ingredients to represent Christ and his 12 apostles, whilst a garland of holly on top of the finished pudding depicted the crown of thorns, and a splash of flaming brandy, the Passion.

Like the Irish barmbrack bread, the habit of adding small trinkets into the mixture was thought to help predict the future of those who found them in their portion, with coins representing wealth, a ring foretelling that the finder would marry, whilst a thimble signalled thrift and a wishbone, good luck.

Enabling us to soak up the true Christmas atmosphere with perhaps the most famous fictional description of the aromas of plum pudding, Charles Dickens sets the scene in his 1843 novel, *A Christmas Carol:*

> A great deal of steam! The pudding was out of the copper. A smell like a washing-day! That was the cloth. A smell like an eating-house and a pastry cook's next door to each other, with a laundress's next door to that! That was the pudding! In half a minute Mrs. Cratchit entered – flushed, but smiling proudly – with the pudding, like a speckled cannon-ball, so hard and firm, blazing in half of half-a-quartern of ignited brandy, and bedight with Christmas holly stuck into the top. O, a wonderful pudding!

The novel also recognises that not everyone was a fan of Christmas traditions. Before Ebenezer Scrooge sees the error of his ways, he announces, 'Every idiot who goes about with "Merry Christmas" on his lips, should be boiled with his own pudding, and buried with a stake of holly through his heart. He should!' Bah, humbug Ebenezer!

Along with the many other Christmas culinary choices was the important decision of which meat, fowl or game bird should grace the festive table. *The English Woman's Domestic Magazine* provided an array of articles and advice on cookery and domestic issues. One of its earliest columns enlightened the reader as to the virtues of the turkey as the main dish for the Christmas lunch, explaining, 'Prominent in our list of Christmas delicacies, the turkey, in the estimation of many, stands unrivalled, and on this account we shall treat how to cook and carve it'. Directions and diagrams were given and, although roast beef and roast goose served with oyster stuffing continued to be popular throughout the Victorian era, the turkey soon became the bird of choice during Christmas festivities.

Chapter Six

Domestic Duties: Life in Service

*Training ... In its broadest and best sense, it is knowing what to do,
and when and how to do it.*
(Robert Wells, *The Bread and Biscuit Bakers and Sugar Boiler's
Assistant*, 1890)

The employment of servants to carry out housework and other menial tasks has long been the preserve of the upper classes and aristocracy. The number of domestics employed depended upon the wealth and income of the family. Those at the top end of the social scale could delegate their duties to a whole household of staff, from rearing their children to scraping their boots and serving their daily meals. Well-off middle class families also tried to create an air of gentrified living by employing one or two servants to help with their own household demands.

In 1861, the census showed that artist and painter William Morris employed a small team of domestic staff to tend to the needs of his growing family, with groom Thomas Reynolds responsible for the horse, wagonette and stable, whilst the household was presided over by cook Charlotte Cooper, who at 27 was seven years older than her mistress. In her 2005 biography *William Morris and Red House*, Jan Marsh notes that, 'Housemaid Jane Chapman laid fires, heated water, made beds, cleaned floors, served and cleared meals, scoured the pots and fetched in the coal'. A little later, Elizabeth Reynolds, a private nurse from Leyton in London, was employed to look after the Morris children.

For the middle classes, the ability to afford live-in help was seen as a status symbol, but they did not have the same household space to distance themselves from their servants as in the large mansions of the upper classes, with their separate servants' quarters. As a result, the domestics and their female overseers lived in close proximity. Surprisingly, the social standing of their employer could be a cause of snobbery amongst domestics. After all, working for a lord was much better than working in the household of a merchant, and often determined the wages and privileges they were likely to receive.

In 1825 former butler and housekeeper, Samuel and Sarah Adams published *The Complete Servant*, an advice manual for both employers and their servants on how to maintain a well-run kitchen, house, stables and garden. The authors give a glimpse of how working relationships could develop in the preface, where they describe their lives and experiences before and after marriage:

> The author, educated in a foundation school, entered service as a footman, in 1770, and during 50 years he served successively as groom, footman, valet, butler, and house steward. His wife began as a maid of all work, then served as housemaid, laundry maid, under cook, housekeeper and lady's maid, and finally, for above 20 years, as housekeeper in a very large establishment.

As well as defined separate living areas to denote the distinction between staff and employees, uniforms visibly identified the domestic and his or her role within the household. Women tended to wear long, plain dark coloured dresses, or white blouses with long, belted skirts protected by an apron, depending upon their role. Hair was neatly tied back, and low-heeled shoes were essential for the long hours they spent on their feet. Male servants wore smart livery, or a simple dark coloured suit, white shirt, tie and black shoes.

A Tax on Servants

In the late eighteenth century the population was growing at a steady rate and domestic servants accounted for a large proportion of the workforce. Their hours were long, their wages were low and the standard of their living quarters varied. Their sole aim was to please their master or mistress sufficiently to keep their job and earn a few pounds a year; if they did not, they could face instant dismissal and even homelessness. Some female servants in this situation might find themselves forced into prostitution, if alternative employment was not forthcoming.

The number of servants within an establishment depended upon the size of the house in which they were employed. Female servants carried out unskilled housework as parlour maids, chambermaids and housemaids, ensuring that beds were made, chamber pots emptied, fires were stoked, and sitting rooms were dusted and prepared for the family. In the kitchen, a scullery maid would carry out all the cleaning, scrubbing and pot-washing required by the cook.

Male servants were employed in cultivating the land, animal husbandry and work that required experience and craftsmanship, often acquired through apprenticeships. Inside the house they might find work as butlers, footmen, page boys (trainee footmen) and lamp boys who prepared and lit the candles, oil lamps and gas lights around the house.

The Servant Tax, introduced in 1777, was proposed by Lord North and aimed at wealthy households employing male domestic servants such as butlers, coachmen and gardeners, but excluding farm labourers, shop and factory workers. Paid by employers at the rate of approximately one guinea per male servant, it effectively reduced the amount of male servants employed inside the household and the domestic burden of lighting fires, hauling water for baths and the numerous list of kitchen tasks were relegated to the realm of women's work.

The tax formalised the relationship between male servant and employer and in some ways instilled the idea that employers 'owned' their servants. This was suggested in T. Henry Baylis's 1857 book *The Rights, Duties and Relations of Domestic Servants and their Masters and Mistresses*. Baylis argued that, 'Servants are bound to give up their whole time to their masters or mistresses, and to obey all their lawful orders in relation to their employment'.

In Scotland, taxes on female as well as male servants were assessed between 1785 and 1792. These Servant Tax Rolls provide a fascinating insight into where most domestics were employed in the latter half of eighteenth century Scotland. In 1785, of the 15,000 servants assessed, 40 per cent of female servants worked in towns, compared to only 18 per cent of males. Each record includes the location of employment, the name of the master, and usually the name of the servant.

Working Women: The Lives of Victorian Servants

Born in 1877, Louise Jermy published her own life history, in which she described her career as a domestic servant. She began her training at the age of 11 in the family home and became a live-in servant from the early 1890s until her marriage in 1911. When Louise left her job to set up her marital home, domestic service was still the biggest employer of women in Britain.

Louise found her various positions by registering with a servants' employment agency. Young women once viewed these agencies as a last resort, due to their dubious reputation. This was a prime area for fraud, and preying upon the desperation of the unemployed, some unscrupulous agencies were known to print fliers listing situations vacant and then charge inflated fees for non-existent jobs, so many women preferred to seek reliable employment by word-of-mouth.

But the constant demand for willing and capable workers meant that agencies became increasingly professional and began providing a businesslike attitude to the world of domestic employment. In 1829, Dr William Kitchiner remonstrated about the employment of illiterate servants and advised in his manual, *The Housekeeper's Oracle*, 'Hire no servant who cannot read or write'.

Many young women like Louise saw domestic service as not only a chance to develop their skills, but also as a refuge from an unhappy home. By showing loyalty and commitment, they hoped to establish a new life, an air of respectability, broaden their horizons and make new friends. Over the next few years Louise was employed in a series of short-term live in jobs, taking temporary and permanent placements as well as working as a cook. Such was the demand for competent domestic servants, that Louise – like many other single women whose confidence came with experience – could gradually choose the roles she wished to take on for their convenience rather than on wages alone.

Published in 1934, Louise's book, *Memories of a Working Woman* claimed in the foreword to be: 'the first autobiography written by a Women's Institute Member'. The Women's Institute's *Home and Country* magazine, in which it was serialised, described the memoir as 'a human document of the early experiences of Louise Jermy's life in service'.

Victorian Domestic Life

In the period from 1841 to 1901 Britain's population exploded from 27 million to over 41 million. Towns and cities had a high concentration of inhabitants as people moved away from the countryside to find work, creating a new Victorian urban culture. In rural areas, the landowning aristocracy continued to enjoy a comfortable lifestyle on their farms and country estates, while those who made money in manufacturing and other industrial ventures were quick to invest in land and enjoy the benefits of the country life.

Domestic service was a natural career option for working class girls. For their employer, having a large number of servants was in itself a status symbol. Glanusk Park was one of the largest late Victorian households in Powys, Wales, and is recorded in the 1891 census as employing 17 servants, ranging from Bertha Elizabeth Storrs, a 42-year-old governess from Switzerland to Emma Souster, cook, and her kitchen maid, Mary Pepper. More extensive properties in England could employ well over 100 servants at any one time. On his Ashridge Estate in Hertfordshire, the Duke of Bridgewater was known to have retained 500 staff, whilst at Eaton Hall in Cheshire the Duke of Westminster employed in excess of 300 domestics to carry out tasks both inside and outside his magnificent home.

For the servant, their position usually offered a certain amount of security and the chance of training to improve their standard of living. Although the work ensured a roof over their heads and a steady wage, they were also at the mercy of their masters and young female servants were especially vulnerable. Some employers and senior male servants took advantage of naïve domestics. Pregnancy was cause for immediate dismissal, and a 'fallen' servant would have been left unemployed, homeless, with no references, and a bleak future ahead of her.

Writing in 1894, George Moore was one of a number of authors who portrayed the life and hardships faced by the Victorian 'fallen woman' in his novel, *Esther Waters*. Originating from a poor working class family, pious young Esther finds work as a kitchen maid but is seduced by the footman. Upon finding herself pregnant – and deserted by her lover – she is told by her employer, Mrs Barfield, 'My poor girl! You do not know what trial is in store for you'. Yet despite her sympathetic attitude, Mrs Barfield dismisses Esther, explaining, 'I couldn't have kept you on, on account of the bad example to the younger servants'.

However, there were rare occasions when love blossomed between master and servant. Sir Harry Fetherstonhaugh of Uppark in Sussex, became besotted with his dairymaid Mary Ann Bullock. Despite opposition, and the 50-year age gap, the pair married and had 21 years together until his death, aged 92. Similarly, in the late 1860s, Edward Seymour, the Earl of St Maur and heir to the Duke of Somerset, began an affair with his kitchen maid, Rosina Elizabeth Swan. He took her with him on his travels and their first child, Ruth, was born in Tangier before they returned to Brighton where they also had a son, Harold. When Edward died prematurely from a emergency tracheotomy shortly after his son's birth, he had ensured that his children were handsomely provided for. Yet, Harold was never able to prove that his parents actually married, so was unable to inherit his grandfather's dukedom.

BROOKE'S SOAP.

4d. a large bar.

The World's most marvellous Cleanser and Polisher. Makes Tin like Silver, Copper like Gold, Paint like New, Windows like Crystal, Brass Ware like Mirrors, Spotless Earthenware, Crockery like Marble, Marble White.

Sold by Grocers, Ironmongers, and Chemists. If not obtainable, send 4d. in stamps for full-size Bar, Free by Post, or for 1s. three Bars (mentioning this publication) to

BENJAMIN BROOKE & COMPANY,

36 to 40, YORK ROAD, KING'S CROSS, LONDON, N.

Advertisement for Brooke's Soap from *The Girl's Own Paper*, 1890. (*Author's collection*)

(*Above*) A postcard showing a family in a Victorian farm kitchen, circa 1900. (*Author's collection*)

(*Below l-r*) A successful harvest meant that hay-making was a time for celebration; Life for the rural cottager centred on the kitchen (Illustrations from *The Girl's Own Paper*, 1889). (*Author's collection*)

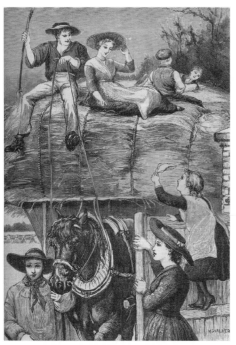

(*Right and below*) Advertisements published in *The Girl's Own Paper* during the 1890s. (*Author's collection*)

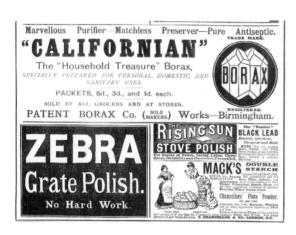

(*Right*) Malt Vinegar – A Myriad of Uses, *The Girl's Own Paper*, 1889. (*Author's collection*)

(*Left*) Lipton – The People's Food Provider, *Illustrated London News*, Now 1895. (*Author's collection*)

(*Above*) From the cook to the scullery maid, each member of the kitchen staff had a specific role (*The Girl's Own Paper*, 1882). (*Author's collection*)

(*Below*) A 'Wilson' portable cooking range (*Illustrated London News*, 1895). (*Author's collection*)

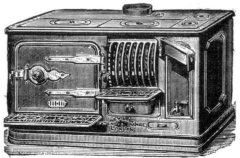

THE 'WILSON' PORTABLE COOKING RANGES,

With Lifting Bottom Grate for Regulating Size of Fire.

☞ Awarded the Gold Medal at the Universal Cookery Exhibition, Portman Rooms.

21 PRIZE MEDALS.

The most Durable, Economical, Simple, and Efficient Range in the Market.

PRICE-LIST POST FREE.

They are Portable, cannot get out of order, will Cure Smoky Chimneys, and have larger Ovens and Boilers than any others.

THE WILSON ENGINEERING CO., Lim., 227L, High Holborn, London.

'Come Stir the Christmas Pudding': An annual festive tradition (*Illustrated London News*, December 1893). (*Author's collection*)

(*Above*) A page from a housekeeper's account book, written in 1863, for a property in Ashby, Northamptonshire. (*Author's collection*)

(*Below*) A cook's accounts and list of food suppliers from 1871. (*Author's collection*)

(*Above*) The kitchen staff and gardener in the scullery of a large house at Fornham St Martin, Suffolk. (*Author's collection*)

(*Below left*) A late 1880 'Wilson' cooking range with double oven; (Below *right*) In the Victorian kitchen there was a tool for every task, from pastry preparation to grinding coffee beans (*Mrs Beeton's Book of Household Management*, 1888 edition). (*Author's collection*)

The " Wilson " Cooking Range.

Utensils used in Making Pastry, &c. 77

THE "WILSON" COOKING RANGE.

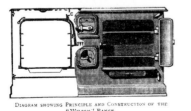

DIAGRAM SHOWING PRINCIPLE AND CONSTRUCTION OF THE
"WILSON" RANGE.

(*Above*) Afternoon tea was a ritual enjoyed by upper and middle class Victorian women (*The Leisure Hour*, February 1892). (*Author's collection*)

(*Below left*) 1890s photograph of domestic staff: The cook relied on the gardener to supply the kitchen with seasonal produce; (*Below right*) Food items of value were kept under lock and key and dispensed by the housekeeper. (*Author's collection*)

THE HOUSEWIFE.

TEA TALK.

'Tea Talk': Illustration from *The Girl's Own Paper* (1893). (*Author's collection*)

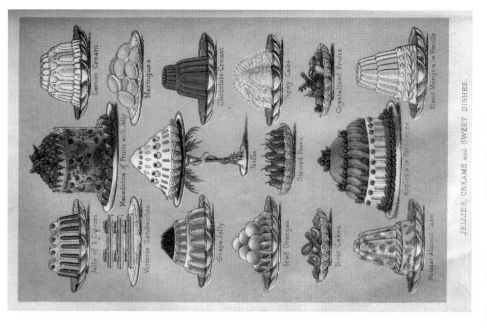

JELLIES, CREAMS and SWEET DISHES.

Lemon Cream.
Meringues.
Chocolate Cream.
Tipsy Cake.
Crystalized Fruits.
Blanc Mange à la Vanille.
Macédoine of Fruits with Jelly.
Trifle.
Stewed Pears.
Ryhlax là la Parisienne.
Jelly of 2 Colours.
Victoria Sandwiches.
Grape Jelly.
Iced Oranges.
Boar Cakes.
Nougat Almond Cake.

SUPPER DISHES.

Pheasant.
Oyster Patties.
Brawn.
Russian Salad.
Tongue Garnished.
Game Pie with Jelly.
Lobster Salad.
Pigeon Pie.
Grayfish.
Roast Fowl.
Shrimp Patties.
Savoury Jelly à la Bellevue.
Galentine of Veal.
Ham Garnished.

Engravings showing jellies, creams and desserts, and supper dishes from *Mrs Beeton's Book of Household Management* (1888 edition). (*Author's collection*)

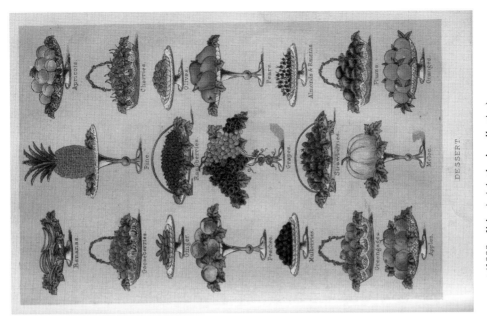

DESSERT.

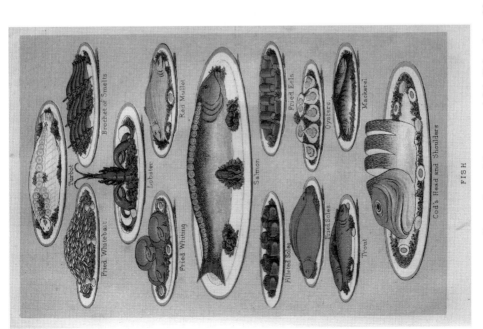

FISH

Engravings of desserts and fish dishes from *Mrs Beeton's Book of Household Management* (1888 edition). (*Author's collection*)

(*Above*) Fine dining: the upper class dinner party (*Punch* magazine, 1882). (*Author's collection*)

(*Below*) A Victorian supper table arranged with a wealth of cutlery, crockery and glassware to accommodate 16 guests (*Mrs Beeton's Book of Household Management* 1888). (*Author's collection*)

SUPPER TABLE WITH FLORAL DECORATIONS, ARRANGED FOR 16 PERSONS

(*Above*) 'Lunch for the Shoot' (*Punch* magazine, October 1882). (*Author's collection*)

(*Below*) 'Mappin and Webb for only the best Sterling Silver and Silver Plate ware' (*Illustrated London News*, June 1900). (*Author's collection*)

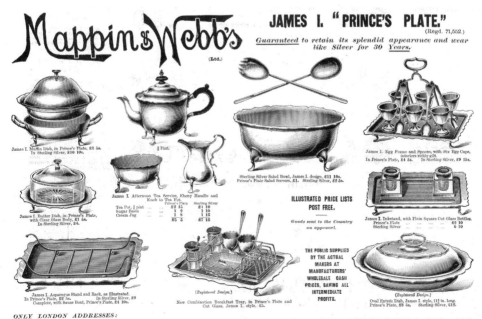

APPRECIATION

THE FAT OFF THE LEAN

Postcards depicting the professional male chef at work, published circa 1900. (*Author's collection*)

THE "PISTON" FREEZING MACHINE

(ASH'S PATENT).

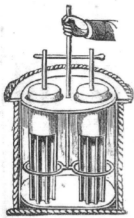

ASH'S "PISTON" FREEZING MACHINE is the most effective and economical method of freezing known. It is rapidly becoming a part of the "cuisine" in the establishments of the aristocracy of this country; it has received the highest patronage, and is used in all parts of the World. By this process Ice Creams are frozen in shapes ready for Table—an operation never before accomplished—entirely superseding the use of icepots and moulds; it also forms a Wine Cooler, and produces Blocks of Ice. When not used with the usual ice and salt mixture, as on board ships, in the tropics, &c., ASH'S FREEZING POWDERS are most effective, and guaranteed to succeed.

Price of the Machines, from 50s. each.

ASH'S FREEZING POWDERS, 34s. per cwt.; or in Boxes at 11s., 22s., and 40s. each.

The "Piston" Freezing Machine. Freezing and Moulding Dessert Ices, Icing Wines, and Making Block Ice.

The "Piston" Freezing Machine (without the Fittings), forming a complete Wine Cooler.

THE SELF - FEEDING REFRIGERATOR.

Patented by Mr. CLARKE ASH.

Awarded the only Prize Medals and Diploma of Honour for Domestic Refrigerators at the Great International Fisheries Exhibition, 1883, *and Health Exhibition,* 1884.

By this invention Economy in Ice, increased space, an uniform low temperature, and ventilated dry atmosphere are attained. Whether the ice placed in these safes be much or little the same low temperature is produced and moreover the lowest temperature generated by any given quantity of ice is maintained day by day until the ice is dissolved. *Descriptive Catalogue free by post.*

PERFECTION IN THE ART OF MAKING COFFEE.

ASH'S "KAFFEE-KANNE,"

(Used in Her Majesty's Household),

Is an entirely new invention for making Coffee in perfection *hitherto unknown.*

PRICES IN BLOCK TIN: 1-pint, 6s. 6d.; 2-pint, 8s. 6d.; 3-pint, 10s. 6d. 4-pint, 12s. 6d.; 6-pint, 16s.; in Electro-Plate from 40s.

The above Patented Inventions are Manufactured solely by

THE "PISTON" FREEZING MACHINE AND ICE CO.

301 and 303, Oxford Street, London.

New kitchen gadgets designed to make the cook's life easier were constantly appearing on the market during the nineteenth century, like this 'Piston Freezing Machine', advertised in 1888. (*Author's collection*)

From Photo by Cassell & Co., Lim.

A BOARD SCHOOL COOKERY CLASS.

Many people will be surprised to learn that cookery classes are so well established in any of the London Board schools as our view shows is clearly the case at the Kilburn Lane centre. The photograph was taken in the midst of the morning's work. Twenty-four girls attending the Kilburn Lane School, all with neat pinafores on, form the class. Half of them—the girls to the right—are occupied in copying recipes; while the other dozen are busily engaged in preparing various homely dishes suitable for an artisan's dinner. The expert teacher has spent the first hour of the morning in explaining how the work is to be done, and the young plain-cooks-in-the-making are now showing in practice how far they have mastered their lesson.

(*Above*) Cookery class at Kilburn Lane Board School, 1899. (*Author's collection*)

(*Below*) Ayton Cookery School in Yorkshire, c.1900. (*Author's collection*)

AYTON SCHOOL.—COOKERY SCHOOL.

But in general, rules were strict; not only banning intimacy between male and female staff, but also regarding insubordination and good conduct. Theft and dishonesty were naturally grounds for dismissal, but other offences, such as drunkenness and even breaking a household item, could result in the loss of wages or even their position, depending on the severity of the housekeeper's rules.

Perks of the Job

Despite the exacting standards and backbreaking work performed by the domestic servant, there were undoubtedly advantages to the job. The cook was in the ideal place to benefit from any kitchen leftovers. Excess produce, rabbit skins, meat bones and beef dripping, along with any bonus goods she received from suppliers, could be sold on to top-up her wage. In some cases, a commission was charged by the cook of one shilling in each pound on the various bills paid to the tradesmen. Employers tended to keep a keen eye on cooks who took liberties by over-ordering supplies for personal gain, which could lead to unpleasant disputes between both parties. *Dickens's Dictionary of London*, written by Charles Dickens's son in 1879, warns: 'Dripping, perquisite for which all cooks will make at least a fight ... Give good wages, and let it be clearly understood before hiring that no perquisites are allowed'.

Lady's maids received cast-offs from their mistresses, such as small accessories, ribbons for their hair, and even bottles of perfume for tasks well done or assistance beyond the call of duty. When the house had visitors the domestics might be lucky enough to receive a small tip from the guests upon departure, boosting their yearly income.

Some servants, who provided a lifelong service were left a small inheritance in the will of an employer. Yet, in an era before state pensions, servants faced an uncertain future and were encouraged to save for their old age. In 1861, the Post Office introduced savings accounts specifically to encourage young servants to buy stamps for their account books.

Domestic Hierarchy: Servants' Roles

Running a household required organisation and efficiency, so it was essential that a chain of command was respected and adhered to at all times. The larger the house, the greater the quantity of employees needed to staff it.

The Butler was aware of all household activities. He took charge of the male staff, a role he presided over from the butler's pantry, where he also gave out his orders for the day. His was a responsible post and not only required him to organise the staff but also to oversee and stock the wine cellar, and take care of the porcelain, cutlery, glass and silverware. He would supervise his footmen in the mammoth task of cleaning the silver, to ensure that the tureens, candelabras and serving salvers were free from tarnish and looked their gleaming best when taken into the dining room.

The Housekeeper was in charge of all the female staff. Upon her person she would carry a bunch of keys which gave her access to the high value areas of the linen closet, china cupboards and stores. Reflecting her status, the housekeeper would usually have the privilege of her own sitting-room near to the storeroom, which she would keep locked and guard with a watchful eye. During the nineteenth century, commodities such as sugar, tea and spices were extremely expensive and kept under lock and key until they were required. She would measure out what was needed and keep accurate records of supplies, ready for reordering.

As senior members of the household, the butler and the housekeeper would be answerable to the steward, who was overseer of the whole estate and took his orders directly from the master. This can be seen on the employment card of a Mrs Frances Burgess Stent, who was the housekeeper of Hardwick Hall in Derbyshire. The card states that her superior is the 'Butler/Estate Manager' and her subordinates are 'All House Staff'.

In some establishments, the role of housekeeper and cook was combined. When this did occur, great responsibility was placed upon the individual, resulting in a lot more work and a greater variety of tasks for them to carry out. If there was a butler, the housekeeper would be seen as the senior member of the female domestics, if not, she was the head of the household staff, directly answerable to the master, or mistress.

Most domestics applied for their positions through agencies, local advertisements, or were recommended by word-of-mouth through others already in employment. But this was not always the case. When Queen Victoria's reign was in its infancy, another woman's fascinating story was coming to its end.

Born in the 1760s, Chloe Gambia was sold into slavery as a small child. Her life was to change considerably when she was bought at a Liverpool slave auction by the Aston family of Cheshire. Taking the little girl under their wing, they took her back to their home, the country estate of Aston Hall. Here, they had her baptised at St Peter's Church in the local village of Aston by Sutton, under the name of Chloe 'Gambia', in reference to the country where she was thought to have originated from.

In March 1807, the Abolition of the Slave Trade Bill was passed in Parliament, paving the way to finally make slavery illegal in 1833. The Aston family continued to give Chloe a home, initially seeing her as a playmate for their children and, once she came of age, enabling her to become a respected and trusted member of their domestic staff.

Chloe was undoubtedly grateful for the opportunities and roof over her head that the Aston family provided, as she remained loyal to them throughout her life. Her diligence saw her rise to become the highest ranking female servant in the household, when she was given the coveted role of housekeeper, overseeing the running of the kitchens, stores and ultimately the smooth operation of the hall and its staff.

On 12 September 1838, after 70 years with the only family and home she had ever known, Chloe passed away. Aston Hall no longer exists, having been demolished in 1938 – one of so many British country houses now lost forever. But the story of this black woman, who made such an impression upon the Astons in her youth, and who eventually presided over the running of their home in adulthood, was immortalised in the graveyard of St Peter's Church. A large gravestone lies in a quiet corner, and along with the names of three other long-standing servants who died at intervals during the late eighteenth and early nineteenth centuries, her inscription reads: 'Chloe Gambia, a Negress who died at Aston Hall on 12th of September 1830 aged 77 years or thereabouts. She had lived in the Aston family 70 years'.

The Cook ruled the kitchen and, although the butler and housekeeper had ultimate authority below stairs, the kitchen was her domain. Decked out in her uniform of white starched cap and apron, worn over a black or grey dress, the cook's first job of the day after cooking breakfast was to meet with the mistress of the house to discuss the menu. She would be expected to work within a budget and buy the best cuts of meat, fish and vegetables available. As well as creating the meals for the family above stairs, she was also required to manage the staff meals, usually taken communally around a large wooden table below stairs. The best cooks possessed diverse skills, enabling them to conjure up everything from elaborate feasts for visiting aristocrats to simple fare for the hungry workforce.

Working days would have been long and exhausting, but most Victorian cooks ran their kitchens with an iron fist and were respected for it. In *Private Life in Britain's Stately Homes,* Michael Paterson describes a notice revealing the cook's authority in the kitchens at Rockingham Castle in Northamptonshire: 'No person Whether belonging to the Family or Not is ever under any pretext to enter the Kitchen without obtaining leave. RING the BELL'.

A strict work ethic was the key to success and recognition in the Victorian kitchen. Born in 1867 in Leyton, Essex, Rosa Ovenden's determination enabled her to climb the domestic ladder from maid-of-all-work to cook to royalty. The opportunity arose for her to learn French cookery at a time when Parisian cuisine was seen as extremely fashionable amongst Victorian society and Rosa's developing culinary skills saw her enjoy a successful career, catering for some of Britain's wealthiest aristocratic families.

At Arlington Court near Barnstaple in Devon, Mrs Hale Parker was the cook to the Chichester family during the 1870s. She, like many other cooks at this time, would have committed most of her recipes, required weights and measures to memory, with new dishes that she wished to try or test out added to the kitchen recipe book. Previous cooks to the Chichester family had captured their culinary knowledge in a notebook dating back to 1863 and Mrs Hale Parker made her own additions in 1876. These included her recipe for the now classic Victoria Sandwich, named after Queen Victoria, which was baked in a square tin, before being sliced across the middle, filled with jam and then cut into fingers to serve to the children in the nursery.

After breakfast, the cook would begin by creating a menu for the day's luncheon and dinner, ready to submit to the mistress of the house for her approval, taking into account any seasonal fruit and vegetables that could be acquired from the kitchen garden and any leftover items which needed to be used. At this meeting, any alterations or requests would be made before preparations would begin. After giving instructions to her kitchen maid, she would write out orders for the tradesmen and spend the remainder of the morning making soups for the following day, or jellies, creams and pastries. Her busiest time would be between the hours of 5pm and 9pm, when she would make final adjustments and dish up the dinner in readiness for transportation to the dining room.

When they finally sat down, the cook and her kitchen staff often ate their meals in the kitchen rather than the servants' dining hall. This was a bone of contention with the other servants, who suspected they might be getting better food.

The Egerton family of Tatton Park in Cheshire were just one of the many grand households who employed a French chef to work in their kitchens, towards the end of the nineteenth century. At this time tastes and fashions were heavily influenced by the dishes created across the Channel. Whilst in large houses, the cook or head chef's work would concentrate solely on creating meals for both the family and the staff, in smaller abodes, the style of cooking would be very different and much less complicated. The cook might be expected to include cleaning and scullery work in her daily list of requirements.

In Mark Forrester's *Pictorial Miscellany* (1855), a poem entitled 'The Song of the Discontented Cook' gives us some insight into the demands of a cook in a smaller establishment, who was expected to constantly multi-task:

> *Oh, who would wish to be a cook,*
> *To live in such a broil!*
> *With all one's pains, to cook one's brains,*
> *And lead a life of toil?*
> *'Tis, "Stir the pudding, Peggy,"*
> *"And give those ducks a turn;*
> *"Be quick, be quick, you lazy jade!*
> *Else one or both will burn."*
> *An hour before the rising sun*
> *I'm forced to leave my bed,*
> *To make the fires, and fry the cakes,*
> *And get the table spread.*
> *The breakfast's scarcely over,*
> *And all things set to rights,*
> *Before the savoury haunch, or fowl,*
> *My skill and care invites.*
> *And here I stand before the fire,*
> *And turn them round and round;*
> *And keep the kettle boiling —*
> *I hate their very sound!*
> *And long before the day is spent,*
> *I'm all in such a toast,*
> *You scarce could tell which's done the most*
> *Myself, or what I roast!*
> *'Tis, "Stir the pudding, Peggy,*
> *And give those ducks a turn;*
> *Be quick, be quick, you lazy jade'.*
> *Else one or both will burn."*

Responsibility and pressure went hand in hand with the job, however, and in return for her proficiency and expertise an established cook could expect to earn a good income. A wages book held at the Berkshire County Record Office shows how the annual income of the cook at Milton Manor rose steadily by approximately £1 per year, from £11 in 1845 to £14 in 1848, but this was still much less than the housekeeper, who was earning a consistent £25 over the same period. By comparison, the combined cook/housekeeper at Lamport Hall in Northamptonshire was earning between £30 and £36 over this time frame, with the help of a kitchen maid and dairy maid, both on £9 per year, and a laundry maid, at £11 per year.

Servants would often move around to achieve better wages, acquire a higher-ranking position or simply to work for an employer with a superior social status. Vacancies were advertised in the newspapers and journals of the day with interviews held at employment agencies specialising in domestic service positions. An advert in the *Edinburgh Evening Courant* of January 1867 states:

> Wanted – A good Plain Cook. None need apply who cannot produce satisfactory testimonials as to character and showing that she has been some years in a good situation and thoroughly understands her business.

In the same year, *The Times* placed an advertisement for a household seeking, 'A good cook in a gentleman's family ... who understands the dairy and baking ... and with no objection to living a few miles in the country'. Another offered prospects for 'The Cook or Housekeeper to a single gentleman, a respectable person with no objection to the town or country, nor to go abroad'.

Advertisements sometimes specified an age range and the need for personal references from previous posts. The wages given and the type of household they would be expected to cater for might also be listed. Some even stated the particular needs of the employer, such as 'baking but no dairy', or included the added bonus that there were 'no knives, forks or boots to clean', intimating that there were others to do this work.

The Kitchen Maid was employed to assist the cook. Rising at 6am she would ensure that the kitchen was ready for the day's activities, before preparing breakfast to be taken in the servants' hall at 8am. She was expected to cook the vegetables, create the sauces, roast meats, make the rolls for breakfast and the cakes for tea, alongside preparing the servants' dinner upon the cook's express instructions. She was expected to learn, and learn quickly. Depending upon the size of the household, the more experienced kitchen maid would be seen as the cook's second.

The Scullery Maid performed all the rough work. Her days were long and hard and included scrubbing floors, washing dishes, skinning game and plucking poultry. Her hands would be chapped from being in water for most of the day, or sore from plucking the feathers from the game birds. There was nothing glamorous about her job, but if she was sensible, she could work hard to gain promotion to the position of kitchen maid.

May Bailey, a scullery maid at Wentworth House in South Yorkshire recalls:

> There were these huge pans, set pots they called them. Like cauldrons, they were ... They had all these big cookers like barbecues. The fires were underneath the grate, with the stoves on either side, like an Aga ... They'd have 20 woodcocks in a row, all hanging down over the fire. The bacon was grilled in another part of the kitchen and there was one chef who had to make all the dishes.

There might be dozens of staff within the household whose meals would be catered for and taken in the servants' hall. A myriad of other servants might be considered necessary. In more affluent households, a lady's maid attended to the mistress of the house, helping her to dress and arrange her hair, while the valet laid out clothes and helped the master of the house to dress. Lower down the scale were page boys and bakers, hall porters and wine butlers. Hardwick Hall employed an 'Odd Man', a position filled at one time by 67-year-old Mr Hetherington, who had formerly been a hall boy. He was expected to complete all the odd jobs, which consisted of refilling the kitchen coal scuttles, assisting the housemaids to lay fires in the rooms and carrying breakfast and dinner trays upstairs and downstairs to the nursery.

At Welbeck Abbey, the Duke of Portland employed engineers and firemen to maintain his steam heating and new electrical system, whilst his wife – like many wealthy women – required a personal maid, and his daughter, a tutor and French governess. Country houses employed legions of outdoor workers to enable their estates to function. The Duke of Bedford was known to have had 60 indoor staff alongside an army of gardeners to tend the grounds and grooms for the horses.

Amongst his many strange rules and demands was the requirement that all parlour maids should be over 5ft 10in. But he was not alone with his unusual requests; other houses were known to have enforced the height restriction on certain staff, footmen in particular, some even paying the individual according to their height.

Along with the permanent employees, the staff of visiting guests also had to be accommodated, and take their meals in the servants' hall. In July 1894, the Prince of Wales, (later Edward VII), visited Penrhyn Castle in North Wales for a four-day house party. Along with 35 other house guests, who all brought their own servants, the cook and her kitchen maids had their work cut out to ensure that everyone above and below stairs was catered for.

Case Study: Erddig Hall

Set in the rolling countryside, two miles from the Welsh border town of Wrexham is Erddig Hall, originally the seat of the Yorke family. Erdigg passed into the hands of the National Trust in 1973 and today this beautiful property and its treasures give an insight into not only the lives of the family but also those of the servants who worked there.

From the eighteenth century through to the Victorian era and well into the first decades of the twentieth century, the Yorke family had a tradition of capturing their servants' likenesses, first in portraits and later in photographs. Descriptions of their characters were often recorded in poetry. Erddig's collection developed into one of the country's most unique archives on domestic staff and helps us to understand what was required to enable a stately home of this magnitude to function.

In 1852 and again in 1912, a photograph was taken of a selection of the staff, posed on the steps in front of Erddig. It was requested that each servant should hold an object in front of them that would later give viewers a clue as to their role within the house. The housekeeper held a bunch of keys, the laundry maid held ironed linen, a footman showcased a silver salver on which calling cards would have been placed, the cook held a kitchen utensil and even the kitchen gardener got in on the act with his watering can.

A study of the 1851 census shows Mary Webster, a widow, aged 42, who, like all the other domestics employed at Erddig, is listed simply as a 'House Servant'. She is the first servant recorded under the names of the family, which would be consistent with her role of cook, putting her high up in the domestic hierarchy. Without prior knowledge of the areas in which the domestics were employed, it can be difficult to distinguish between their roles. By the 1861 census, much more detail had been added. In the kitchen, Mary Webster, now aged 52, is recorded as born in Knocking, Shropshire, and she is officially listed as the cook, with 20-year-old Charlotte Allmond from Flintshire providing help as the kitchen maid and Margaret Jones, born in 1823 in Llangollen, employed as the dairy maid.

The census helps us to follow Mary's career and, by 1871, she has the combined role of housekeeper and cook, which was common practice at this time. Her original kitchen and dairy maids had moved on, perhaps to get married, and had been replaced with Ruth Davies and Hannah Richards, two young girls starting their adult lives as domestics on this great estate.

When Simon Yorke II took over Erddig he continued the tradition set by his father and commissioned a series of portraits of his servants before his death. These were all male employees, however. With the arrival of photography, images of the cook, housekeeper and housemaids gradually began to appear, with a daguerreotype created in 1852 of Mary Webster, who went on to have a long career with the family.

She was so well thought of, that a verse describing her character was created to 'immortalise' her culinary prowess by Philip Yorke II:

> *Upon the portly frame we look*
> *Of one who was our former cook …*
> *She knew and pandered to our taste*
> *Allowed no want and yet no waste.*

Two handwritten recipe books from the Erdigg kitchens survive from the Victorian era. As Harlan Walker reveals in *Cooks and Other People*, 'the first was begun in 1839 by Victoria Cust, then aged 15, who was to marry Simon Yorke III; the second is begun by her, but then moves into another hand, probably that of her daughter-in-law, Louisa, who married Philip II in 1902'. Harriet Rogers was chosen to succeed Mary Webster in the role of cook and housekeeper at Erddig, but when she left to become lady's maid to the Yorke sisters, she took her recipe books with her.

Household Accounts

Despite such a large percentage of Victorian Britons being employed in domestic service, very few personal memoirs produced by servants survive. Yet, this dedicated workforce has not been forgotten and recollections have found their way into letters, postcards, documents and diaries. By piecing together these snippets we can tell their stories and understand a type of employment now virtually lost forever. Household account books can help to outline the duties of the domestic servant and the tasks they were expected to carry out. Typically these were lined notebooks, with columns in which to write the date, a description of each commodity or service and the price paid it.

Even Mrs Beeton impressed the importance of this record-keeping upon her readers:

> A necessary qualification for a housekeeper is that she should thoroughly understand accounts. She will have to write in her books an accurate registry of all sums paid, and for any and every purpose, all the current expenses of the house, tradesmen's bills, and other extraneous matter.

An account book from a country house in Ashby, Northamptonshire, seems to have been completed by the butler, housekeeper and the cook, providing a concise journal of expenses and a glimpse into the day-to-day running of an upper class household. The entries begin with the note:

> *Christmas Gratuities for December 1862*
> *Gave Lamplighter 2s 6d*
> *2 Postmen 5s*
> *Dustman 2s 6d*

For this household postage was a big expense, with numerous letters sent on a weekly basis and correspondence for Switzerland and Geneva hinting at connections abroad. Entries for envelopes, sealing wax and stamps appear on nearly every page. Railway charges were a monthly occurrence, for both travel and for the delivery of hampers containing supplies, though we can only guess at what sort of treats these would have contained.

Toothpicks at 1s 6d, a mustard spoon costing 6s and a corkscrew were among the smaller items purchased for the dining room, whilst references to furniture oil, wash leathers, knife powder and lamp cottons confirm that cleanliness was a constant battle. On 2 April 1864 three bottles of blacking, costing 4s 6d, were bought as part of a regular, order necessary to keep the kitchen range in pristine condition.

Each month, a tally of the wages paid to servants was also recorded. There was no regular pay date, and it seems that the staff in this particular establishment could go from seven days to four weeks before receiving their money.

<u>*Wages and Board, 25th of May 1863*</u>
To Wm Stead	£1, 8s
Edward	£1, 8s
Charles (12 days)	£1, 4s
Thomas (1 wk)	14s
Self	£1, 8s

Reliable suppliers, as well as servants, were essential for the smooth operation of the household. The cook could source seasonal produce from the kitchen garden, but she also needed other commodities to create the vast array of dishes expected. Long before the introduction of the supermarket, individual retailers would specialise in specific products; the surnames of the regular suppliers and the weekly spend with each one were listed in the account book for 1868:

May 4th–9th	Lamport – Meat and Poultry	£6	2s	8d
May 11th–16th	Lamport – Meat and Poultry	£2	12s	8s
May 18th–22nd	Lamport –Meat and Poultry	£3	5s	6d
May 1st	Groceries	£1	6s	10d
May 4th	Groceries for Ashby & Side of Bacon	£3	5s	5d
May 26th	Groceries and Brushes for Ashby	£1	3s	2d
	Spiking for Bread	£2	16s	2d
	Worsdale Greengrocer	£1	17s	3d
	Gilson Fishmonger	£4	10s	5d
	Whitfield Fishmonger	£4	18s	–
	Dilley – Milk and Cream	£4	13s	3d

Food supplies bought separately for special dishes, or to replenish stocks, were added individually:

11th April 1864	A whole Stilton Cheese	10s	6d

The cost for the repair of the key for the back door was noted, and even the arrival of a new staff member: 'On Saturday, March 2nd 1872, Mrs Roberts came as housemaid. Wages – £17 including £1 washing money. Board and wages with vegetables'. It is also possible to learn more about the employer from the notes written in the account book where items particular to the master or mistress of the home were recorded:

13th June 1863	*Opera Hat*	–	*2s*	*6d*
5th April 1864	*Theatre Tickets*	*£2*	*12s*	*6d*

It is surprising just how much information can be gleaned about the operation of one household from a few simple pages of notes.

An Organised Workforce

To ensure that the household ran like clockwork, every servant knew their place, where they should be at all times, and the task that they were expected to carry out.

No matter how strict the rules, working as a domestic servant during the Victorian era had more benefits than working as a factory hand, dock worker, or farm labourer. There was sometimes the opportunity to climb up the ladder but, most importantly, the jobs were often permanent and came with housing, food and clothing in the form of a uniform, although many had to buy this with their own wages. In some houses the domestic staff wore different coloured uniforms to distinguish between their roles, so that laundry maids, kitchen maids and still room staff could be seen at a glance. This also ensured that they were visibly going about their duties in the right place at the right time. To reflect their status, the housekeeper and the cook wore an outfit suitable for their position, and the male staff wore smart liveried uniforms.

A standardised dress code was also a way of disguising individual personalities, with the black dress, white apron and frilled cap – a Victorian creation. In some cases, both male and female servants were also given new names to make them easier for employers to remember, but sadly removing their identities to fit them into the well-oiled machine of domestic service.

On large estates married workers might be offered a cottage, whilst those who had been with the family for most of their lives might be given a place to live upon retirement. Generally, servants employed in larger properties ate well, were decently clothed and warm. Some suffered from ailments linked to their work, such as arthritis, or 'housemaid's knee', a condition brought on by the continued scrubbing and cleaning carried out while on their knees. Many well-off employers would have provided access to a doctor, who would have been able to treat or manage such illnesses. It was in the interest of the employers to maintain clean and healthy domestic staff to ensure they got the best possible service from their workforce.

A good position enabled a domestic servant to see another side of life from the restricted one they may have grown up in as rural cottager, and in some instances, when employed as a lady's maid or valet, they may have had the chance to travel abroad with their employer. During the Victorian era, there were thousands of employment agencies offering domestic work on all levels, allowing the worker to improve their position, should they wish to, or escape from a bad employer. All they needed were good references.

'Domestic service is not without its prizes', wrote Emma Brewer, in an article entitled 'Our Friends the Servants', published in *The Girl's Own Paper* in June 1893. She continued:

> it is no small encouragement to a girl beginning life to know that although she may commence service in the meanest situation and by performing the roughest possible work, yet that by the exercise of self-discipline, industry and attention she may in time reach the highest rung of the ladder of domestic service and this realises a great deal that a good woman values on which it has been her great object to attain.

Not all servants were lucky enough to work in a large, stately mansion with the camaraderie of others and most tended to work as a lone member of staff in a middle class home. This could be a very lonely life indeed, with long hours and an extensive list of duties to carry out during the working day. Even Mrs Beeton acknowledged the difficulties involved in the role of maid-of-all-work, in her *Book of Household Management*:

> The general servant, or maid-of-all-work, is perhaps the only one of her class deserving of commiseration: her life is a solitary one, and in, some places, her work is never done. She is also subject to rougher treatment than either the house or kitchen-maid.

One maid-of-all-work, Hannah Cullwick entered domestic service in the early 1840s at the age of eight. In later life she often moved from job to job to try and alleviate the monotony of her domestic work. From her mid-twenties, Hannah detailed her life in service in the form of a diary, at the request of her lover, and later husband, Arthur Munby, a solicitor, poet and civil servant, who was fascinated by working women.

A typical entry in Hannah's diary highlighted the drudgery faced by domestic servants:

> Open'd the shutters & lighted the kitchen fire ... Made a tart & picked and gutt'd two ducks and roasted them ... Clean'd the steps & flags on my knees ... Wash'd up in the scullery. Clean'd the pantry on my knees & scoured the tables.

Second Homes and Country Estates

Some aristocratic families possessed, along with their English estates, additional properties by the coast, or north of the border. A Scottish retreat provided a rural getaway, where hunting, shooting and fishing parties could be enjoyed. The family and some of the key staff might decamp there for a few weeks in the summer, and such trips were not unusual for wealthy aristocrats with considerable means.

The second home was unlikely to have a full complement of domestics, so various members of the household would be taken along to ensure that their every need was catered for. For the kitchen staff, the menu could be adapted to include regional dishes to feature the game birds and venison shot on the estate and the freshly-caught salmon and trout from the estate's rivers and lakes.

In the interest of self-sufficiency, large estates often had their own mills, providing flour for baking, and their own farms, where cattle, pigs, sheep and poultry would all be bred for the table. Others went a step further and set aside a building for their own brew house. Gallons of beer were consumed by the servants during the early part of the Victorian era – coining the phrase 'one over the eight', meaning one glass of alcohol too many would render a person drunk. The beer produced was not particularly strong, roughly one or two per cent proof, but in the mid-1800s cholera was rapidly spreading across Britain in contaminated water supplies, so drinking beer, which had been purified and fermented, was a much safer option.

Feasts Fit for a Queen

Queen Victoria, Prince Albert and their family travelled extensively during her reign, regularly staying at some of Britain's most notable stately homes and castles. Her arrival had usually been planned months in advance, with every last detail taken into account. Most elaborate preparation went into planning the meals she would be served during her visits. The cook and her staff would create magnificent banquets – each course a work of art – with hours of preparation going into each and every dish. Surviving account books reveal the cost of ingredients needed, the increased meat and game ordered and the copious amounts of alcohol brought in to tend to the royal family's every need.

Every courtesy was shown to the monarch by her hosts, who went to great pains to make sure that each dining experience ran like clockwork. In *Queen Victoria at Home*, Michael De la Noy gives us a glimpse into her true dining preferences. It seems a typical meal enjoyed by the monarch at Windsor in 1897 consisted of 'soup, fish, sirloin of beef, a sweet and dessert. Claret and sherry were poured by a piper; Champagne handed round by Indian servants'.

Interestingly, Reginald Brett, later 2nd Viscount Esher, made a note in his diary about an occasion on which he and his wife were invited to dine with Queen Victoria. There were 'No courses', he wrote. 'Dinner is served straight on, and when you finish one dish you get the next, without a pause for breath.' It seems that dining was not always a sedate affair, and when in the presence of a monarch with a healthy appetite you had little option but to keep up with her majesty!

Careful records were also kept detailing the type of food consumed in the royal servants' hall. In 1866, when it was 'not a pudding day', the servants at Windsor Castle were instead given soup created with 50lbs of stock made from rice, barley, peas and, occasionally, a 'mutton reduction', along with vegetables from the garden. Also recorded was the amount of cutlery and crockery required for the 78 staff at Balmoral, the 94 staff at Osborne House and the 161 at Windsor. Preparing a meal for the staff was a mammoth operation, not only requiring skill and foresight, but also organisation on a grand scale.

To ensure that mealtimes for the family, guests and staff went off without a hitch, it was essential to employ competent staff. A letter from the master of the household to the keeper of the privy purse, dated May 1854, discusses the requirements necessary to become a second master cook in Her Majesty's kitchens. For a salary of £145 per year with board, the chef in question would preferably be a Frenchman, or a 'foreigner' who could also speak English. Taking direction from the chef de cuisine, he would be expected to undertake all aspects of creating a dinner, even though his area of expertise was the entrées. When the chef de cuisine was away, catering for the Queen in either Scotland or the Isle of Wight, the second master cook would be required to run the kitchens, and therefore, have needed experience of successfully managing staff under him. It was insisted that the applicant was not less than 30 years of age.

Interestingly, this document also gives us an insight into some of the kitchen staff already employed, listing alongside the chef de cuisine, four master cooks, yeomen cooks, assistants, pastry cooks and apprentices. Compare this to an extract from an Establishment Book detailing the servants employed in the confectionery, pastry and bake-house sections of the Lord Steward's Department in 1897 and you can see what a wide range of skills were needed to meet the daily catering requirements of the reigning monarch and her lifestyle.

Case Study – From Service to Science Fiction

Set high upon the South Downs of West Sussex, Uppark has a Georgian interior filled with treasures collected by the Fetherstonhaugh family during their Grand Tour of Europe. In the nineteenth century, later generations made their own improvements, adding stables and kitchens as separate buildings connected to the main house by tunnels.

Between 1850 and 1855, Sarah Neal was engaged as housemaid to Lady Fetherstonhaugh's sister, and while working for the family she met Joseph Wells, a gardener who was employed on the estate. In 1853, the pair married and four children soon followed. The last child, a son whom they named Herbert George Wells, was to be greatly influenced by his time at Uppark. Sarah and Joseph left Uppark to set up a shop selling china, but when the business failed Sarah was forced back into service at Uppark. Now in the role of housekeeper, she held the position from 1880 to 1893.

Although Sarah and her husband were now living separate lives, her youngest son was allowed to stay with her. Herbert would have spent many hours in the kitchens and staff quarters of Uppark, witnessing the hustle and bustle of his mother's life in service. One entry in Sarah's diary hints at just some of the issues she faced, 'Worried with the Cook leaving, how unsettled this house is'. But Sarah's position also enabled her to pull strings, allowing her son access to the books in the family library. The stories within inspired Herbert's later prolific career as the science fiction writer H.G. Wells, and, in a way, his mother's domestic service had allowed him a window to another world.

Kitchen Life and Layout

Staff were never allowed to enter the house through the front doorway of the property in which they worked, but instead, had their own entrance at the back. Often this was located near to the storage areas, where wood and coal were kept. The positioning of the kitchen within the household was always given serious consideration. Some houses boasted enormous kitchen areas, enabling a wide variety of dishes to be created at the same time; large hearths, roasting ranges and spits allowed sides of beef and whole piglets to be cooked; on the hobs, stock pans, stew pans and fish kettles jostled for position.

Each part of the kitchen was dedicated to a specific task, all of which created steam and odours that were not to be discernible to those above stairs. The noise and smells from the kitchen were not permitted to linger, or permeate into the dining room. Serving hatches were kept closed when not in use, and there were some occasions when the kitchen door was covered with a heavy baize material to prevent culinary odours seeping through.

Strong-smelling vegetable water was disposed of as soon as possible, and heaven forbid that any food or fat was burned, as the oven would have to be cleaned and fumigated at the earliest convenience. Where possible, high windows – often requiring rods to open them – were installed on the north or western walls, allowing ventilation and lowering the temperature within the kitchen. Stone flooring and glazed tile walls helped keep the room cooler, and lofty stone ceilings went some way to protecting the rooms above should a fire break out in the kitchen, yet also allowing steam to rise and odours to disperse.

By the nineteenth century, most kitchens were situated in basement areas, or within a separate wing of the house, helping to keep kitchen activities behind-the-scenes and the servants out of sight. Upstairs and downstairs households were segregated by the maze of corridors and stairways, which linked the grand rooms from the working areas of the house. Situating the kitchen further away from the dining room was not without its drawbacks, and keeping the food warm could often be a problem. Although the meals were piping hot when they left the care of the kitchen, their long journey through the draughty corridors meant that large metal dish covers were essential to protect the food on the platters beneath – the added weight and unusual proportions making them a heavy load for the footmen and serving maids to carry.

The film *Gosford Park* gives a visual example of the layout below stairs in a large stately home. It not only shows the separate dining arrangements of the cook and the rest of her team from the other domestic servants, but also how each room leading off the main kitchen area was designated for a specific purpose.

The Scullery

The Victorian attitude to hygiene is thought to have been 'cleanliness is next to godliness', and certainly servants used whatever facilities available to keep their surroundings spotless at all times. They worked hard to reduce the smell of bad odours, keep vermin, beetles and bugs away, and, in turn, deter the spread of disease. Coal fires and kitchen ranges created steam and dirt and required intensive labour to keep them clean.

Maids cared for the fires and lighting within the house. The kitchen range was completely cleaned out every day, with damp tea leaves often scattered over the fuel to reduce the amount of dust when raking out the ashes and cinders. The cinders were sieved from the ashes, to be reused later in the kitchen. The oven was swept out, grease was removed and the cast-iron parts of the range were black leaded and polished ready for the cook's inspection.

Large houses used the kitchen solely for cooking and had a room set aside for washing-up, known as the scullery. It was lined with plate racks and dominated by a wooden or stone sink, where the washing of crockery and scrubbing of pots and pans took place. In the late 1880s, young Emily Harris worked as a kitchen maid at Warwickshire's Weddington Castle. A dinner party for 18 people could generate up to 500 separate items of china, glassware, kitchenware and cutlery, which all needed to be cleaned, and one of Emily's jobs would be to ensure that every piece was washed, dried and spotless, and ready for the cook the next time she required them.

In most sculleries, a large table provided the perfect work surface where vegetables could be peeled and chopped, and fish and game plucked, gutted and prepared. Steam from boiling coppers filled the air, providing water for both cooking and cleaning purposes but requiring constant mopping and tidying to keep the area safe to work in.

A mixture of soda and soft soap was used for washing up, which made a creamy cleaner able to remove grease, whilst polishing compounds were used to scour brass and tin utensils, and pots. Manufacturers soon began to see the benefits of creating household products that made the job that little bit easier. Blacking and black lead were available to polish cast-iron kitchen ranges; knife powder sold in packets helped to give cutlery that extra gleam; beeswax, purchased per pound, gave new life to wooden objects; and a whole range of soaps, pastes and polishing powders removed tarnish and deterred corrosion.

The Still Room

The still room was originally added to the kitchen layout back in the seventeenth century. It was a special place where alcoholic waters, medicines and even perfumes were distilled and infused with herbs, flowers, fruit, or vegetables from the kitchen garden. Small copper stills allowed dry ingredients to be steeped, before being slowly heated to add flavour and taste to the resulting brew. Initially, these concoctions were used mainly as medicines for ailments such as juniper water, or gin, which was once believed to be a cure-all for epilepsy.

Here in the still room, you might expect to find a drying stove. At no bigger than a foot square, its metal-runged grilles enabled slices of orange and lemon, which had been soaked in syrup, to be slowly dried out and turned into candied peel to use as an ingredient, or decoration, in other dishes. At the height of the Victorian era, the still room would have been buzzing with activity, as the kitchen staff preserved and pickled surplus fruit and vegetables from the garden, to enable them to be used out of season. Sizeable estates not only had the family to feed but also an army of servants, so it was important to make ingredients accessible all year round. Nothing went to waste, and preserving whilst the produce was in abundance during the summer was an economical measure.

Greatly influenced by British connections with the Empire, the Victorians began to reproduce recipes that originated abroad. Chutney, also known as Chatney, from India became a much loved accompaniment to meals and was another way of using up surplus produce. As early as 1845, Eliza Acton explained how to create these relishes in her book *Modern Cookery for Private Families*. 'All Chatneys should be quite thick', she told her readers, 'almost of the consistence of mashed turnips or stewed tomatoes, or stiff bread sauce. They are served with curries; and also with steaks, cutlets, cold meat, and fish'.

The traditional Asian and Indian varieties of chutney consisted of either a wet, or dry, selection of ingredients combined into a complementary mix of flavours. Early British expatriates relied on this preserved form of foodstuff and the Royal Navy even saw the benefits, when they adopted lime pickle and chutney into the sailors' rations to help ward off scurvy. But when spices became more accessible back in Europe, these Indian dishes were adapted to suit Western tastes. Easily made from fruit or vegetables, sugar, vinegar and spices, the Victorian cooks experimented with their own concoctions from the produce available from their own kitchen gardens and hot houses.

With the expansion of industry and overseas trade, great changes were on the horizon. The same products that were once pickled and preserved on a smaller scale in the still rooms and home kitchens across the nation were now manufactured, so many of the bottled sauces and chutneys could be sold ready-made. As a result, the end of the era saw the role of the still room diminish, as the requirements of the kitchen altered.

The Laundry

The laundry was responsible for ensuring that all the household clothing, linen, tablecloths and napkins were pristine. The work necessary to achieve this was backbreaking and the laundry maids would think nothing of carrying dozens of buckets of water in from the yard to fill the laundry copper, which heated the water for washing.

Working 12-hour days – like most other servants, with only a half-day off a week – the laundry staff had a set list of tasks for each day. Monday and Tuesday were usually washdays, involving exhausting, hot and steamy work. From Wednesday to Friday, mountains of ironing, starching, folding and airing needed to be carried out, before the weekend arrived and the dirty washing was sorted out, ready to begin the weekly routine again.

In the early part of the Victorian era, the dolly peg and tub replaced the old wash board and, instead of scrubbing the dirty washing against the board to try and remove the dirt, the clothes were placed in a soapy tub of water and agitated with the dolly peg, a long wooden pole with four legs on the end, which helped to pound and swirl the washing clean. This was another long and laborious task.

Box mangles were wooden contraptions used in larger houses to iron sheets, tablecloths and any other large flat items, which would otherwise have taken a very long time to remove the creases with a flat iron. As large as a long narrow table, the device comprised a wooden box weighted down with dozens of stones, which helped the rollers beneath to move over the laundry and flatten it. Box mangles usually required three employees to work successfully.

* * *

Domestic service during the nineteenth century was extremely hard work, and particularly demanding for those employed in roles within the kitchen. The prospect of marriage might entice a kitchen or scullery maid away from her situation, but for women who rose to the higher status roles of cook or housekeeper, the respect that their position commanded made it very difficult for them to give up their independence. It even prompted some to choose their career over having a family of their own.

Chapter Seven

Culinary Creativity

Cookery, in our era, has been thought beneath the attention of men of science; and yet, was there ever a political, commercial, or even a domestic event, but what always has been, and always will be, celebrated either by a banquet or a dinner?
(Alexis Soyer, *A Shilling Cookery for The People*, 1854 edition)

The amount of food and drink consumed by guests during a formal dinner or weekend country house party could be astronomical. The cook's ability to order the correct quantities of ingredients and work out amounts and portion sizes was one of the most important tasks she had to perform. She also had to be versatile and find innovative ways of presenting the same base ingredients in a new format.

During the shooting season, pheasants, partridges and guinea fowl were brought to the table on a regular basis and the cook was challenged to create tempting variations for the guests. Her skills were expected to extend to an endless repertoire of fabulous dishes for every occasion, with recipes ready to call upon at a moment's notice. From fancy entrées to elaborate centrepieces requiring hours of preparation, knowledge and experience was essential.

The level of thought that went into each dish was astounding. Even a vegetable as simple as asparagus received careful consideration. Cooks usually boiled asparagus in a copper pan, as the harmless chemical reaction between the vegetable and the copper pan gave the cooked asparagus a greener appearance, making it seem more attractive when served.

The cook also had to oversee the more basic preparations. No matter what size the kitchen, a stock pot would be constantly cooking. Poorer families used the stock pot to eke out the smallest morsels of meat, boiling animal bones to make a tasty broth. The bones would enrich the liquid and, although the finished soup contained more vegetables than meat, at least the flavour would be there. For those existing on a small income, soup from a stock pot provided a whole meal, but for the wealthy, soup was just one of the many courses to be enjoyed as part of a long and elaborate dinner. Within a large kitchen, a simmering stock pot ensured there was always a base for sauces and stews, or to enhance other dishes. The most common use of a stockpot was to make a *consommé* – a clear soup that would stimulate, rather than overload the appetite in preparation for the meal ahead.

To create the *consommé*, first onions, leeks and a *bouquet garni* of herbs would be added to water. Beef on the bone or even a whole fowl would be used to create an intense flavour. This would be allowed to simmer slowly for a few hours, before the fat was skimmed off the top and the meat and vegetables removed. Clarifying then took place by adding egg whites and passing the mixture through a fine mesh until the liquid ran clear. To complete the *consommé*, the reduced stock would be diluted and the seasoning adjusted before tiny pieces of vegetables were added to the golden liquid for a garnish.

Pastry Perfection

One of the ways in which a Victorian cook would show off her artistic flair was to use pastry as a decorative device. There was no such thing as a simple pie crust – the top had to be embellished. A very robust pastry made using more egg yolks in the mix allowed the cook to cut, carve and mould the dough around a variety of ingredients. Intricate wooden borders would be used to create fancy edges on pies, pastries and edible feats of engineering, encasing all manner of fillings. Minute hand stamps of flowers, flourishes and motifs would enhance a design even further, before the pastry was slowly baked to keep its shape and structure.

A shortage of wheat in the latter part of the eighteenth and early nineteenth century resulted in the cost of flour rocketing. In an effort to economise, households began to make their pies without a top crust, to limit the amount of pastry they used. Pottery manufacturer Josiah Wedgwood seized on this idea and began to market pie dishes with decorative covers, to make the open pie look appealing when served on the table. One of these innovative designs was even exhibited at the Great Exhibition in 1851.

Depending upon their income, some people chose a base and cover in a simple beige pottery known as 'cane ware', often resembling a basket design, whilst others went for elaborate, brightly-coloured earthenware dishes, known as 'majolica'. These mimicked the decorative cheese dishes of the day and were lavishly ornamented with fish, rabbits and farmyard animals – to depict the type of meat contained within the lidless pie beneath.

Offally Good

In architecture, fashion, garden design and many other areas the Victorians created distinctive new styles and this approach was no different in their culinary creations. But they also had a love of thrift and enjoyed the challenge of using every last scrap of food to produce something worthwhile. Where meat was concerned, cooks used all sections of the carcass to create as many dishes as possible.

The nineteenth century cook was therefore adept at devising dishes out of the least appetising ingredients. Offal – the internal organs and entrails of a butchered animal – was commonly incorporated into pâtés, soups, and stews. As we have already discovered, the Scottish were well-known for using a mixture of sheep's liver, heart, and lungs in their recipes for haggis, but other areas had their own particular preferences. Faggots – originating from the East Midlands – were made from minced pig offal and wrapped in the thin membrane of caul fat which surrounds the pig's stomach organs. Black pudding, a Lancashire favourite, consisting of oatmeal and pig's blood shaped into sausages and encased within a pig's intestine, made a tasty addition to the English breakfast, alongside the traditional lamb's kidneys cooked in a spicy sauce – a method known as devilling.

Not just the preserve of the poorer classes, the calf's head could also be made into a dish enjoyed by the wealthy. The head was boiled until tender and dressed with a sauce made out of the minced brains. The tongue would have been removed, sliced and placed on the serving platter around the head, along with the eyeballs, which were classed as a rather gruesome delicacy. Pressed ox tongue was sliced and served in sandwiches.

It was not the cow, however, but the pig whose bodily parts inspired the widest range of dishes from each cut of pork. The pig's head would be used for making brawn (jellied pig's head), the snout might be served boiled and the pig's cheeks cooked slowly in a rich gravy. From the neck end, fore loin and middle loin, chops could be cut, or sections of the joint could be boned and rolled for roasting or braising. Underneath, an area known as the tenderloin could be roasted, braised, or sliced for frying, while the back legs offered the perfect solution for a large roast joint, providing lean and tasty meat.

Even the undercarriage of the pig was not put to waste and the belly pork – fatty yet moist – compensated in flavour for what it lacked in meat. The meat on the foreleg and the lower foreleg, known as the hock, required longer, slow cooking and was the ideal meat to use in stews, whilst the gelatine provided by pig's trotters, once boiled, could be added to pork pies, and the trotters themselves coated in breadcrumbs and served as a dish in their own right.

Delectable Desserts

'The dessert crowns the dinner', declared Eugene Briffault, food journalist and author of *Paris a' Table* in 1846. He continued:

> To create a fine dessert, one has to combine the skills of a confectioner, a decorator, a painter, an architect, an ice-cream manufacturer, a sculptor, and a florist. The splendour of such creations appeals above all to the eye – the real gourmand admires them without touching them!

The Victorian cook certainly had a challenge on her hands. Some of the finished dishes were real architectural masterpieces, taking a great deal of thought and artistic skill to construct and requiring numerous ingredients at every stage of preparation. Extremely labour intensive to create, every detail was thoroughly planned, so that each course not only tasted delicious, but also smelled appealing and looked attractive.

To make some tasks less daunting, the cook would often turn to her culinary moulds. Copper moulds were regularly in use in larger kitchens, whilst housewives tended to lean towards the earthenware varieties, which were increasingly popular towards the end of the nineteenth century. A professional cook would delegate the laborious task of preparing tiny pieces of vegetables or fruit to her kitchen maids, ready to decorate savoury potato dishes and pates, or sorbets, ices and puddings, which were initially fashioned using a mould into various shapes, from simple rings and terrine style bricks to elaborate fishes, rabbits and dessert style domes.

Highly fashionable Belgrave moulds enabled complex jelly shapes to be made into desserts to grace the table at the end of a meal. Two-toned effects could be achieved, as the construction of the Belgrave moulds provided cavities within the jelly which could be filled with fruit juices, rose water, or blancmange. Before the advent of the refrigerator, the setting process was helped along by placing the full mould into a bowl of ice and leaving it in a cool place for a few hours. To remove the finished work of art, the mould was dipped in warm water and shaken gently to release the wobbly pudding. Sitting proudly on a serving dish, it might be further embellished with sprigs of mint, raspberries, strawberries, or regimented rows of grapes. The uncontrollable wobbly nature of this dish would have provided additional amusement for the guests.

In the mid-1800s, cabinet pudding was a popular dessert. A combination of sponge cake, glacé fruits and macaroon biscuits were added to a mould, before a home-made custard was poured over the top to soak in and solidify the ingredients. This was then steamed before the domed pudding was turned out and finished with a rich alcoholic sauce.

The Dining Experience

Mealtimes were extremely important in the Victorian household – custom and decorum always had to be observed. Any social *soirée*, lunch, or dinner was considered a formal occasion. Guests were expected to be punctual and for meals taken after 6pm, a dress code was required. During the nineteenth century, the ladies would wear low-necked gowns of silk, satin or chiffon – often designed with short sleeves to complement the accompanying long-sleeved gloves – whilst the men donned fine dinner jackets, waistcoats and black trousers.

Etiquette even dictated the sequence in which the party entered the dining room, with the male host always escorting the wife of a distinguished guest or newcomer to the area, whilst the wife of the host would accompany her husband's business partner, or friend. The remaining guests would follow in accordance with their social standing and rank, with men and women on alternating seats around the table. The lavishly decorated dining room would reflect the fashions of the day, with the emphasis on elegance, opulence and style.

Hand-crafted side tables would showcase ceramic figurines, alongside ornately carved pieces of furniture. Leafy potted plants added a touch of greenery and fine mirrors and paintings would adorn the walls, providing talking points. Even the dining table could be a thing of beauty, often enhanced with an elaborate floral centrepiece, or a stylish arrangement of fruits, bonbons and confections placed to draw the eye. Chandeliers and candelabras added extra light and improved the overall ambiance. Each place setting held an array of silver cutlery and sparkling stemware.

Depending upon the importance of the meal, diners might find up to eight different sets of knives, forks, spoons and their accompanying rests, each with their own special purpose. Game shears, fish knives, melon spoons and lobster forks were just a few of the implements needed to negotiate the endless procession of courses. There would be room for the service plate, topped with a napkin arranged in a decorative design, a bread plate to the left-hand side of the setting and a whole selection of glasses to hold water, wine, sherry or champagne. At larger gatherings a place card would be aligned next to each setting, so that the diners knew exactly where they would be expected to sit.

A typical menu consisted of an appetiser – perhaps of raw or baked oysters, clams on a half shell or even caviar – before a clear bouillon or cream soup, was served. The fish course, along with a small portion of potatoes and light vegetables, would be accompanied by a glass of hock with white fish, or claret with a dish featuring salmon. By the time the party had progressed to the main course of roasted beef, pork or poultry – usually served with green vegetables – another glass of wine would be poured, suited to the flavours of the dish they were eating. A sophisticated dessert, or heavy pudding, would provide a welcome sweet addition to the menu, followed by a cheese board and fresh seasonal fruit. More courses might have been inserted, depending upon the importance of the occasion.

William Makepeace Thackeray described the choice of dishes one could expect to enjoy at the start of a dinner and the etiquette involved in positioning these dishes upon the table:

> The first course consists of soup and fish. Two dishes of fish dressed in different ways – if suitable – should occupy the top and bottom; and two soups, a white and a brown, or a mild and a high seasoned, are best disposed on each side of the centre piece; the fish sauces are placed between the centrepiece and the dish of fish to which each is appropriate, and this, with the decanted wines drunk during dinner, forms the first course.

He explains that these dishes were then replaced 'by boiled poultry, ham or tongue, roasts or stews, etc, and of vegetables, with a few made dishes, as ragouts, curries, hashes, cutlets, patties, etc, in as great variety as the number of dishes permits'.

A dinner party was a fashionable affair and the choice of menu and quality of the presentation would have been paramount to the hostess, and the sole responsibility of her cook. The hostess might relay her observations of food at other dinner parties to ensure that her own dinners were of the finest quality and appearance, and would compliment, or criticise, her cook depending upon the guests' reaction to the dishes served. Although the aim was to impress the diners, choosing quality of food over quantity of courses was a sensible regime preferred by many cooks.

In *Relish*, her biography of Victorian celebrity chef Alexis Soyer, author Ruth Cowen describes just one of the many dinners Soyer presided over in his role as Head Chef of the London Reform Club between 1837 and 1850:

> Then came the dishes for the main service, carefully arranged on the crisp white damask cloths – two, four, or six platters of each item laid out in perfect symmetry. These included a choice of róts, such as young, tender turkeys, no bigger than chickens, their necks skinned but heads left intact, tucked under their wings. There were also hares in a red-currant sauce, capons with watercress, plump white ducklings, spit-roasted and served with the juice of sour bigarade oranges.

Along with dishes sampled at elaborate dinner parties and official functions, the publication of 'celebrity chef' cookbooks, like Soyer's *The Gastronomic Regenerator* (1846), enabled a hostess to replicate these fashionable dishes from the comfort of her own home.

With an extensive programme of important luncheons and dinners to cater for, the menus produced by the royal kitchens often favoured an average of six course meals, where the dishes showed off the calibre and skills of the cooks, chefs and kitchen staff. When the Empress Augusta of Germany visited Queen Victoria at Windsor Castle in May 1879, a dinner was held in her honour, consisting of six courses: a choice of soup, followed by a fish course of whitebait or salmon; escalope of veal provided a tempting *entrée*; roast beef and lamb formed the basis of the main meat course; and an array of tantalising tartlets and gateaux were offered for dessert to complete this well-rounded meal.

Upon completion of the meal, with ample time to allow for digestion and numerous topics of polite conversation, it was customary for the Victorian hostess and the other women in the party to retire to the drawing-room, where a selection of teas and coffee awaited. This allowed the men to remain at the table and enjoy a glass of port or cognac and perhaps a cigar, or withdraw to the library for further drinks and conversation before rejoining the ladies.

Service Etiquette

There were strict rules regarding the service of meals in the Victorian dining room. Nineteenth century Britain was heavily concerned with tradition and there were a number of ways in which dinner guests would receive each course. *Service à la Francaise* was a method evolved from the Middle Ages by the aristocracy, where the only cutlery supplied to the diner was a spoon. Each male guest would bring his own knife, often in the form of a dagger, allowing him to serve himself and any female guests seated nearby. The blade was used to cut the meat from a joint, while the point was used to spear it. An individual's social status, denoted by their position at the table, would determine the food they were given, as not everyone was served the same type or quality.

Although this method of service became more refined with the introduction of cutlery, silver platters, dishes and porcelain, the diner's position at the table still dictated the food they received during the nineteenth century. Like a giant buffet, designed to dazzle and tantalise the taste buds, each course served in this way had a cornucopia of meat and side dishes, all served on the table at the same time, requiring the guest to carve and serve themselves as the plates were passed around.

By the mid-nineteenth century, the *Service à la Francaise* dining experience began to change. The Russian Prince Kourakin introduced a new method, which later caught on in England and formed the basis of the style we still use in restaurants today. Each course was prepared and divided in the kitchen before being placed in front of the diner, enabling the whole party to eat the same dish at the same time. Once finished, these were then cleared and a series of other dishes followed in succession.

Some courses enabled the guest to serve themselves from platters or tureens offered by the footmen, who would appear discreetly at the guest's side. This allowed the diner to decide how large a portion they would take and to avoid offending their hostess by not eating everything on their plate. It is also worth noting that the dining rooms of this period were carpeted to muffle the sound of the footmen's shoes, as they passed continuously back and forth across the floor, attending to each guest. It was considered a breach of etiquette to engage in any sort of conversation with a servant during the meal.

Known as *Service à la Russe*, this method emphasised the pleasing of the palate rather than the eye and, although some dinners could involve over 20 courses, 12 to 14 was the norm. Each was designed to enhance the meal and the dining experience as a whole. Tastes would build in strength towards the highlight of the roast course, before gradually mellowing in preparation for the dessert and the final cheese course, which was thought to aid digestion.

Service à la Francaise had put the importance of carving and portioning the food on the guests, whereas *Service à la Russe* shifted the responsibility to the cook and her kitchen staff, who were required to find an elegant way of presenting the food. Menu planning was paramount, allowing guests to judge the composition of the dinner and engage their appetites; not only the size of each course but also the flavours within them had to be well-balanced.

Gourmet's Glossary

The habit of serving pre-dinner drinks was not established until the very end of the nineteenth century and did not immediately catch on. Even in the Edwardian era it was seen as a relatively new custom. When an accompaniment was needed in addition to the alcoholic beverages, the Victorians turned to France for inspiration:

Amuse Bouche – From the French phrase meaning 'mouth amuser', these one-bite canapés were created to tantalise the taste buds and stimulate the diner's appetite.

Canapés – Decorative food eaten in one bite. Derives from the French word for 'couch', meaning a garnish that sits on top of bread. The base varies to include bread, puff pastry or small crackers, whilst the garnish can include purées, caviar, or a combination of savoury foods or relishes.

Vol Au Vent – Derives from the French phrase for 'windblown', referring to the lightness of the pastry case, which provides an edible container for a sweet or savoury filling.

Hors d'oeuvres – A selection of small appetisers served before a meal, often to accompany drinks, as the guests arrive for dinner.

The Perfect Picnic

Although outdoor eating was already well-established in British history, Queen Victoria made picnicking in scenic locations truly fashionable. Despite being regarded as casual affairs, servants were still in attendance at aristocratic picnics and matters of etiquette were considered. Invitations were sent out beforehand and a great deal of thought was put into the location of the event, ensuring that there were enough shady sites to protect the ladies from the sun. Breathtaking views were essential, but the picnic could not be held on a spot such as the edge of a cliff, as it was not considered polite to alarm ladies of a sensitive disposition.

The servants were sent on ahead, often carrying chairs and tables to set up a home from home experience for the guests, but on most occasions rugs and blankets were laid down, providing comfortable seating. The servants would then withdraw and remain just out of sight, but close at hand should their assistance be required, or until they were needed to clear up the debris and transport the picnic tackle back home.

On this one occasion it was not considered *de rigueur* for the servants to wait upon the gentry, and instead the gentlemen would wait upon the ladies, bringing them whatever they fancied from the vast array of food laid out before them. Initially, it was not the 'done thing' for the men to sit on the ground when the ladies were also seated but, as the decades passed, this ruling seemed to be relaxed.

For the Victorians, being at one with nature did not necessarily mean compromising on dining traditions and they believed that the food should be just as sophisticated as meals eaten in the dining room. Baskets packed with sumptuous treats prepared by the cook and a small army of kitchen staff were arranged by the accompanying maids and footmen. On some occasions a kerosene burner was brought along, enabling a kettle to be boiled to make tea. Homemade lemonade was a popular choice and poured into jugs, along with ginger beer, to quench their thirst on a hot summer's day. For those who enjoyed an alcoholic beverage, a choice of sherry, brandy, claret, white wine and even champagne would also be on offer.

For an example of just how extensive the Victorian picnic might be, Mrs Beeton described a typical menu needed to cater for a large gathering of 40 people in her *Book of Household Management*. Joints of beef, lamb, duck, chicken and ham made up the body of the meal, accompanied by veal and pigeon pies, lobsters, salads, bread rolls and butter. Any cook worth her salt would have included a choice of desserts within the picnic hampers – from cheesecakes and cabinet puddings to pastry tarts and turnovers. Fresh fruit would have been available for those who preferred a lighter option, along with cheese and biscuits to cleanse the palate and complete the feast.

Much forethought was needed when preparing the picnic and, along with the host of cutlery and crockery, a supply of kitchen gadgets were essential to make sure the event ran smoothly. Corkscrews were indispensable for opening not only the wine but also any corked condiments.

*   *   *

Throughout the nineteenth century, the upper classes continued to demand greater variety and complexity from the dishes prepared by their kitchen staff. Although some servants were initially cautious of change, Victorian cooks embraced innovative design, new ingredients and products, and revelled in presenting fresh culinary creations. Victorian tastes had become increasingly sophisticated and diverse. If a new dish, technique or culinary novelty was accepted by the trend-setting higher echelons of society, then the middle classes considered it stylish to follow suit. Versions of the latest dish would gradually find their way on to the tables of their contemporaries and even into the cookbooks of the lower classes.

Chapter Eight

Food from the Empire

When eating fruit, remember who planted the tree;
when drinking water, remember who dug the well.
(Vietnamese Proverb)

British food has always been multicultural. From the influence of the Romans in ancient times, and the French during the Medieval period, the British have developed an eclectic mix of tastes and flavours. Trade with other continents enabled our ancestors to try new ingredients and recipes, and as Britain's Empire flourished, so did knowledge of foodstuffs, as well as the accessibility of exotic spices and increased commodities.

With an empire made up of a series of colonies, protectorates, territories and dominions, Britain once ruled over 20 per cent of the planet before most of its colonies became independent during the twentieth century. From the 1500s, Britain conquered overseas lands desirable for agricultural or mineral wealth, or for strategic purposes. Merchants sent their ships to trade with the West Indies and North America, and shipped goods back to London in the form of sugar, bananas, cocoa, tobacco and a wide variety of items that could not be grown in Britain's cold climate.

The British population had increased from 8.7 million in 1800 to 16.7 million in 1851, reaching just over 41 million by the end of Queen Victoria's reign. The solution to the higher demand for food and agricultural products from this rapidly expanding nation was to import from abroad. The Industrial Revolution had seen the wealth of newly-constructed factories reduce the amount of arable land available for crop growing and cattle rearing, so now Britain turned to its colonies to trade livestock and other food commodities. Expanding shipping lines brought food stuffs from America, Australia and New Zealand, and when the Suez Canal opened in 1869, large amounts of cheap corned beef arrived from Argentina. Once the vessels docked in British ports, the growing rail network was used to transport these goods around the country.

At its peak of trade in the Victorian era, merchants would reload the ships with goods made in Britain's factories, sailing back to different parts of the Empire and ferrying passengers to and from the colonies. British men settled in the colonies to work as administrators, overseers of trade operations or soldiers, but they also carried out lower status labour intensive jobs. Gradually, women began to accompany their husbands, to help them build a life in these far-flung outposts.

Each region's cuisine varied enormously and new cookery techniques were absorbed into the British way of life. Trade routes had long ago introduced Britons to lemons, oranges and limes from Arabia, and cinnamon, cloves and nutmeg from Asia, but those who relocated to these new colonies now had cheap, easy access to these ingredients. When they returned to Britain, they brought the recipes for many of the dishes they had grown to enjoy back with them. Some of the most popular were tantalising curries, laced with spices and served with rice, and delicious chutneys which enlivened meals.

Colonially Creative

Although Mrs Beeton's *Book of Household Management* concentrated on recipes and methods for the British cook, it also provided interpretations of recipes and cookery practices from other countries. As many Victorians were building new lives overseas at this time, homesick housewives would have found her advice invaluable. Mrs Beeton's simple observations enable us to understand some of the challenges female immigrants may have had to experience in their new home country.

Mrs Beeton sympathised with the wives of American and colonial settlers, explaining that the mistress of the house not only had to have a thorough practical knowledge of cookery, but also of household and dairy work. She would need to acquire the skills to make soap, candles, sugar, and other 'household requisites', that their English equivalents with access to well-stocked shops would never dream of making themselves. Interestingly, she also pointed out that English domestic servants were being tempted by higher wages to leave Britain and try their hand at supporting those emigrants who were trying to seek their fortunes overseas.

Mrs Beeton's comparison of the availability of produce in America is interesting. She states that meat in the rural communities is much cheaper and more plentiful than in England and therefore 'wastefully treated'; that fish is a large part of the American diet and in abundant supply; and that 'nearly all the vegetable products of the Earth are to be found in their immense extent of territory'. Bread-making is practised in every household, she claims and the diverse blended flours available enabled the colonists to create products that 'vary the monotony of the household loaf or hot rolls of English breakfast tables'. To overcome the hurdles of acquiring the more expensive items, colonists grew their own rice, tea and coffee, cultivated their own grapes for wine-making, brewed their own beer, and made sugar and rum from sugar cane.

Although Isabella Beeton seems forward-thinking, some of her comments come across as comical today, such as her declaration that 'the idea of sugar being detrimental to the teeth is an exploded one ... it is known that the ice cream and ice cold drinks are very often injurious when partaken of too freely, as is sometimes the case in America'. As far as Australia's culinary reputation went, Mrs Beeton explained that 'to all intents and purposes it is the same as in England except that the same meals served in hotels in Australia would be at two thirds of the cost'.

Mrs Beeton's comments could sway the beliefs of the general public. At this time, tinned meat was being imported from Australia and many Britons were prejudiced against it, but she strongly defended its quality, stating that only the best meat was used for this purpose and even comparing the tinned mutton from Queensland as being in equal condition to the cuts sold in Smithfield Market, London.

The *Book of Household Management* is likely to have travelled far and wide in the luggage of emigrating colonists and, although some of her recipes would not have been practical for British kitchens, the ingredients used in some examples would have been plentiful overseas. 'Soup from Kangaroo Tails' was apparently a hearty dish to serve during the Australian winters; 'Parrot Pie' requiring a dozen paraqueets was depicted in an engraving of the finished dish, garnished with the legs and feathers of the unsuspecting birds; 'Roast Wallaby' was stuffed and trussed in the same manner as a hare and served with the head still on. These dishes may still have raised a few eyebrows when first experienced by the British immigrant.

Life in the British Raj could not have been more different than the conditions experienced by British colonists in Australia. The mistress of the household would have depended upon Indian servants for all her domestic and culinary tasks. Unfortunately, Mrs Beeton does not portray the servants in a particularly good light and advises getting on good terms with the *Khansaman* (cook), who would also be in charge of buying provisions from the bazaar.

Despite never having visited the country herself, Mrs Beeton judged the local beef 'coarse, sinewy and tasteless', stating that 'the mutton is decidedly inferior quality', while 'pork is not eaten in India at all'. Of fruit, she declared that peaches are 'poor', grapes are 'thick-skinned' and comically, that mangoes have 'a taste only acquired by those who have not a strong prejudice against turpentine'. Despite this, she admits that Indian cooks are clever and, 'with very simple materials will turn out a good dinner' and also confesses that their rabbits are 'good in curries', snipe are 'well flavoured' and 'quails are better in India than almost anywhere else'.

She explains the need to boil and filter the drinking water, but adds that 'something' is needed to make it more pleasant to the taste, and that this 'something' often happened to be brandy – 'of which a great deal is consumed in India, to the detriment of the health of the majority'. Consequently, she tries to steer her readers into consuming iced tea or adding lime juice to boiled water.

One particular dish 'discovered' during the days of the Raj and brought back to Britain to be enjoyed at many a country house breakfast, was kedgeree. The combination of smoked fish, rice and hard boiled eggs mixed with a delicately spiced curry powder was, at first, unusual to the British palate. But tastes developed from simple farm-produced dairy products to include more adventurous devilled kidneys and strong tasting kippers, and so kedgeree was soon offered alongside these dishes.

Another popular Anglo-Indian dish that has stood the test of time is mulligatawny soup. Coloured and flavoured with turmeric, then thickened with rice, it was known as 'pepper water' from the Tamil *molegoo* (pepper) and *tunes* (water) before the British added meat (chicken, beef or lamb) to make it a hearty dish for a typical British winter's day.

The British Shopping Experience

For Victorian cooks, shopping could be an exciting affair. The burgeoning nineteenth century railway network meant that food could be transported quickly and enjoyed all over the country, bringing fresh fish from the coast to the rural communities and vegetables from the fields for the city dwellers. Trade brought new and enticing ingredients to stores and shopkeepers wasted no time in advertising the latest products and using them to create decorative displays. Supermarkets were still a long way off, but in the nineteenth century equivalents known as stores, dry goods such as tea and coffee were sold alongside butter, cheese and bacon.

In 1869, John James Sainsbury and his wife, Mary Ann, opened their first store at 173 Drury Lane, London. Initially selling fresh foods, they gradually expanded their range to include packaged goods, served to their customers by staff in white aprons over marble-topped counters. Their motto was 'Quality perfect, prices lower' and their emphasis on cleanliness and excellence attracted a loyal following of shoppers, who were drawn to the variety of products on display. Such was the success of their initial venture that, by the time of John's death in 1928, 128 shops in carefully chosen locations bore the name J. Sainsbury Ltd.

In many Victorian stores, most items could be purchased by weight and individually wrapped at the end of the transaction, but as soon as tinned goods and processed products appeared on the shelves, they quickly became standard household store cupboard items. There were no health and safety or food hygiene restrictions for Victorian shopkeepers, and butchers would happily hang their joints of meat in the shop window, and even outside, making the most of the space they had to draw potential customers in.

For the thrifty Victorian shopper on a budget, markets were essential. In his 1851 book *London Labour and the London Poor*, journalist and social researcher Henry Mayhew wrote a vivid description of the street language which filled the air in the capital's markets:

> The pavement and the road are crowded with purchasers and street-sellers. The tumult of the thousand different cries of the eager dealers, all shouting at the top of their voices, at one and the same time, is almost bewildering. "So-old again," roars one. "Chestnuts all'ot, a penny a score," bawls another. "An 'aypenny a skin, blacking," squeaks a boy. "Buy, buy, buy, buy, buy - bu-u-uy!" cries the butcher. "Twopence a pound grapes." "Three a penny Yarmouth bloaters." "Who'll buy a bonnet for fourpence?" "Pick 'em out cheap here! three pair for a halfpenny, bootlaces." "Now's your time! beautiful whelks, a penny a lot." "Here's ha'p'orths," shouts the perambulating confectioner. "Come and look at 'em! here's toasters!" bellows one with a Yarmouth bloater stuck on a toasting-fork. "Penny a lot, fine russets," calls the apple woman: and so the Babel goes on.

Mayhew's account not only gives us an insight into the noise, and hustle and bustle encountered in a Victorian street market, but also reveals the wealth of products available for sale. Watercress sellers set up their stalls next to shellfish vendors. Bushels of gooseberries and bundles of herbs were sold alongside cobnuts, baked potatoes, and cough drops. Turnips were piled high, walnuts stacked precariously; shrimps, sweetmeats and spice-cakes were all available to those with the wherewithal to purchase them.

In addition to market traders, costermongers sold their wares from barrows both in the markets and in the streets. 'During the summer months and fruit season', Mayhew explained, 'the average number of costermongers attending the Covent Garden market is about 2,500 per market day. In the strawberry season there are nearly double as many'. Similar markets were held across the city throughout the week, with Saturday night markets proving extremely popular for the working class shoppers, who were paid late on a Saturday evening. A visit to a Sunday market ensured that the family would have food on their tables on the Sabbath day.

*   *   *

Immigration greatly influenced food choices and, as families of different cultural backgrounds settled in locations around the country during the nineteenth century, their customs, tastes and traditions seeped into the British way of life. Pockets of varying nationalities sprang up, many seeking refuge from religious persecution or simply hoping to carve out a better life. Jewish and Russian families appeared in cities throughout the era, alongside Italians and Irish families who had fled the famine in their homeland. This often resulted in new food-related businesses appearing, as immigrants fought to scrape together a living.

Mayhew interviewed a number of street sellers during his research. One man explained:

My missis is lame, she fell down a cellar when a child. Last October twelvemonth I was laid up with a cold, which settled on my lungs and laid me in bed for a month. My missis kept me all that time. She was "working" fresh herrings; and if it hadn't been for her we must all have gone into the workhouse.

Similarly, a young girl of about 11, whom Mayhew described as 'stunted and wretched', explained that she was 'sent out by her mother with six halfpenny worth of nuts, and she must carry back 6d or she would be beat'. She could neither read, nor write and, like many other children from the poorer classes, relied upon the sale of food items to provide money for her family.

Sadly, some immigrant streetsellers were looked down upon by the 'regular' costermongers, according to Mayhew:

> Thorough-bred costermongers repudiate those who sell only nuts or oranges in the streets, whether at a fixed stall or at any given locality. They repudiate also a number of Jews, who confine their street trading to the sale of 'Coker-nuts' on Sundays vended from large barrows. Nor do they rank with themselves the individuals who sell tea and coffee in the streets, or such condiments as pea soup, sweetmeats, and the like. I often heard all such classes called 'the illegitimates'.

Despite this, the street sellers in towns and cities continued to peddle their culinary wares to passers-by. From hot eels and chestnuts to crumpets and penny pies, these stalls provided cheap and tasty food. Those living in cramped conditions in the city often had no cooking facilities available to them in their overcrowded dwellings or lodging houses. They relied upon street food for sustenance and could not be too fussy about where it may have originated or how it had been cooked.

To accompany street food, a selection of beverages – not only tea and coffee, but also lemonade, ginger beer, hot wine and milk – helped to keep the shivering customers warm in winter and refreshed in summer. 'Of all elder-wine makers the Jews are the best as regards the street commodity', wrote Henry Mayhew. 'The elder wine urn is placed on a stand covered with an oil-cloth, six or eight glasses being ranged about it. It is sold at a halfpenny and a penny a glass'.

At all hours of the day and night, vendors would work the streets specialising in one particular victual, as Mayhew's interviews with the traders revealed:

> I was told by one who spoke from a personal knowledge, "a pepperminter" had two little taps to his keg, which had a division in the interior. From one tap was extracted "peppermint-water;" from the other, "strong peppermint-water." The one was at that time 1d a glass, the other from 2d to 4d, according to the size of the glass. With the "strong" beverage was mixed smuggled spirit, but so strongly impregnated with the odour of the mint, that a passer-by could not detect the presence of the illicit compound.

These street sellers kept the city poor fed, watered and temporarily warm, and enabled hundreds of others to eke out a living.

Colonial Commodities

Sugar

One of the earliest references to sugar in Great Britain dates back to 1319, when 44 tons were being shipped to London by a merchant from Venice, in exchange for wool. Throughout Medieval Europe, sugar was a costly luxury. Initially sold by apothecaries and used in medicinal remedies for its healing and antibacterial properties, prices continued to remain high, even when it was fast becoming a food staple as a sweetener in tea and coffee.

The growth in British sugar consumption was rapid. In 1700, the amount used in Great Britain alone was 10,000 tons, rising to 150,000 tons by 1800, with a massive increase to almost 1,100,000 tons by the year 1885. By the Victorian period sugar had become affordable to the masses, but this was due to the use of a shameful source of labour. In 1655, Britain took control of Jamaica from the Spaniards and became heavily involved in the sugar industry. The plantations in the West Indies were booming and it was soon clear that more workers were needed to tend and harvest the cane. Slaves were brought in from Africa to prepare the sugar for export, and many were treated harshly, living and working in diabolical conditions.

The use of slave labour and increased production gradually caused the price of sugar to drop dramatically. The British used the ingredient to sweeten their tea, but at first it was purely a luxury for the wealthy and the equipment used to prepare it was of the best quality. Before, sugar was sold in granulated form it was transported in lumps known as sugar loaves. Conical in shape, these could be bought by weight or by the whole cone and broken off in lumps, depending upon the usage. A hammer and chisel would be needed to break the cone up, but for domestic use it was cut using sugar nippers. Similar to tongs, they could be gripped and squeezed, but the addition of blades meant that they could break the sugar lumps into more manageable pieces. The lumps would then be stored in a tin or wooden box to keep them dry. The sugar would have been locked away when not in use and only weighed out by the housekeeper, or mistress.

This simple ingredient had a whole host of utensils for its preparation. Along with the nippers, were tongs for serving and compartmental caddies, which allowed powdered sugar to be stored alongside the lumps. A pestle and mortar was essential for the cook to grind the lumps to a fine powder, and castors to sift it. The tongs, nippers and castors were often made of silver, whilst the boxes used for storage were elaborately carved, or inlaid, decorative pieces of furniture in their own right.

In 1833, Parliament passed the Abolition of Slavery Act, giving all slaves within the British Empire their freedom and paying plantation owners compensation based on the number of slaves they had owned. Sugar production became increasingly mechanised and the once highly-prized commodity became part of the everyday British diet, incorporated into all sorts of confectionery items and increasingly available to the general public.

Coffee

England's first coffee house is thought to have been established in 1650, when a Jewish man named Jacob opened his premises in Oxford, moving to London two years later to repeat his successful venture. Women were initially banned from coffee houses, which were considered purely a male domain. By 1675, there were over 3,000 coffee houses in England and the public continued to flock to them, despite Charles II's attempt to suppress the establishments as meeting places where scandals were born and trouble was brewed alongside the coffee.

Rapidly increasing in number throughout the nineteenth century, in 1867 John Timbs revealed just how popular the capital's coffee houses had become with Londoners, in *Curiosities of London*:

> There are in the metropolis about 1000 Coffee-shops or Coffee-rooms; the establishment of the majority of which may be traced to the cheapening of coffee and sugar, and to the increase of newspapers and periodicals. About the year 1815, the London Coffee-shops did not amount to 20, and there was scarcely a Coffee-house where coffee could be had under 6d. a cup; it may now be had at Coffee-shops at from 1d. to 3d. Some of these shops have from 700 to 1600 customers daily; 40 copies of the daily newspapers are taken in, besides provincial and foreign papers, and magazines. Cooked meat is also to be had at Coffee-shops, at one of which three cwt. of ham and beef are sometimes sold weekly.

Timbs also described the atmosphere and regular customers who frequented some of London's most fashionable 'coffee drinking' haunts. The Jamaica Coffee House in Cornhill 'is noted for the accuracy and fullness of its West Indian intelligence. The subscribers are merchants trading with Madeira and the West Indies. It is the best place for information as to the mail-packets on the West India station, or the merchant vessels making these voyages'. Langbourn Coffee House in Lombard Street 'has a broiling-stove in the coffee-room, whence chops and steaks are served hot from the gridiron; and here is a wine and cigar room, embellished in handsome old French taste', and the Baltic Coffee House in Threadneedle Street 'is the rendezvous of merchants and brokers connected with the Russian trade, or that in tallow, oil, hemp and seeds. The supply of news to the subscription-room is, with the exception of the chief London, Liverpool and Hull papers, confined to that from the north of Europe and the tallow-producing countries on the South American coast'.

During the Victorian era, the Temperance Movement set up coffee houses, intended as alcohol-free places where the working classes could relax and an alternative to the public house. Across the pond, the Union soldiers fighting in the American Civil War were issued with 8lbs of ground roasted coffee as part of their personal ration, to keep them awake and sustained. When supplies became scarce, chicory was substituted to eke out their quotas.

Tea

Initially, tea was marketed as an exotic medicinal drink and, as with sugar, only the aristocracy could afford it or the elaborate serving pieces that accompanied tea-drinking rituals. Tea parties became extremely popular amongst the upper classes, despite allegations by religious reformers that this dangerous brew would bring ruination upon families. Yet when Charles II married the tea-drinking Catherine Braganza of Portugal in 1662, opinions changed and the whole culture of tea-drinking became so fashionable that alcohol consumption went into decline. Tea importation rose from 40,000lbs in 1699 to over 240,000lbs by 1708, and as the craze swept the nation, tea began to be consumed by all levels of society.

There were still those who tried to warn of the recklessness of drinking tea. Irish Quaker and reformer Mary Leadbeater explained the frivolity of wasting money on a beverage that had no nutritional value in her 1811 pamphlet, 'Cottage Dialogues': 'Now if you both take to drinking tea, (and sure you can't sit down to one thing, and he to another,) you must have a quarter of an ounce of tea, that is three half pence at the lowest; and two ounces of sugar, that is three half pence more'.

Shipments of tea continued to be brought to Britain, sometimes taking up to 12 months to arrive from the Far East. When the East India Company gained the monopoly on the tea trade, they followed their American counterparts by designing clipper ships to replace their heavy English 'tea wagons'. The clipper ships could travel at speeds of up to 18 knots, helping to reduce the journey time in bringing this precious cargo to British shores. From Europe, tea was re-exported to America and the colonies.

The Duchess of Bedford, one of Queen Victoria's ladies-in-waiting, is credited with starting the tradition of afternoon tea. Served after 3pm, it was not intended to be a substantial meal, but instead acted as a light refreshment to relieve hunger pangs, restore energy and revive the flagging feeling often experienced at this time of day. Rather than being prepared in the kitchen, afternoon tea served at a country house was usually organised within the still room. The housekeeper would supervise the maids and arrange the correct amount of tea to be added to the pot. Tea was an expensive commodity so, along with the many keys the housekeeper held she was also responsible for the tea caddy, which was always kept locked when not in use.

When the drawing-room bell rang, the teapot would be dispatched with a footman, who would also leave food for the mistress to serve to her guests. Dainty cakes, thinly-sliced bread and butter, usually with the crusts cut off or toasted, were the order of the day. The intention was that the choice should be appetising and pleasing to the eye, but not too heavy. As many women wore gloves or expensive articles of clothing, each morsel would be easy to handle to avoid soiling their garments.

In his 1848 novel, *The History of Pendennis*, William Makepeace Thackeray notes the effects that the drinking of tea has had on polite Victorian society:

What part of confidante has that poor teapot played ever since the kindly plant was introduced among us. Why myriads of women have cried over it, to be sure! What sickbeds it has smoked by! What fevered lips have received refreshment from it! Nature meant very kindly by women when she made the tea plant; and with a little thought, what a series of pictures and groups the fancy may conjure up and assemble round the teapot and cup.

As the years passed, the menu changed to include filled sandwiches of cucumber, smoked salmon, or egg mayonnaise and cress. Hot buttered scones were added, along with more elaborate cakes and sweet treats, but the emphasis was always on bite-size portions.

Outside the home, tea consumption was equally as popular. Coffee houses across the country flourished with the addition of tea on their menus and some even became known as 'Penny Universities', as any man could obtain a pot of tea, conversation and a copy of the newspaper for the price of a penny. The first official tea shop had emerged in 1717, when Tom's Coffee House in London became a tea establishment called the Golden Lyon, where both men and women were welcome.

Today, the plaque outside the shop reveals more of its history:

Thomas Twining (1675-1741) founded the House of Twining by purchasing the original Toms Coffee House at the back of this site in 1706, where he introduced tea. In 1717 he opened the Golden Lyon here as a shop to sell tea and coffee.

In 1787 his grandson Richard Twining (1749-1824) built the handsome doorway incorporating his grandfather's Golden Lyon symbol and two Chinese figures. Twinings is believed to be the oldest company to have traded continuously on the same site with the same family since its foundation.

In fine weather, English tea gardens also provided the ideal place to while away a few hours. Inspired by the Dutch tavern gardens, where innkeepers would serve tea to their guests at their garden tables, the English equivalents became extremely fashionable throughout the nineteenth century and enabled women to socialise in mixed gatherings. Ladies and gentlemen gathered at these early outdoor cafés to consume their beverages in the open air; accompanied by musical entertainment and concerts, they enjoyed chatting to acquaintances, whilst taking a walk through the floral gardens or partaking of a game of lawn bowls. In the tea gardens the custom of tipping developed, when small wooden boxes were left on each table with the letters 'T.I.P.S – 'To Insure Prompt Service' – inscribed on the side.

Chocolate

By the 1650s chocolate had arrived in England, but the huge import duties on cocoa beans of 10-15 shillings per pound, meant that, once again, only the rich could afford it. King Charles II's chocolate-drinking court set the standard and soon speciality chocolate houses began to spring up in London, where people could go and chat, meet friends and drink this new beverage. Samuel Pepys recorded his morning visits to chocolate houses in his famous diary.

Rich and bitter chocolate drinks were sold at the chocolate houses, alongside coffee, snacks and alcoholic beverages and chocolate was also offered in a solid cake format, so that the drink could be made at home. One of the most significant changes to the way the chocolate was consumed occurred when an English doctor, Sir Hans Sloane, was travelling in Jamaica. He added milk to the Jamaican bitter chocolate draught and brought his recipe back to Britain, where he initially sold it as a medicine.

The Victorians enjoyed this discovery in all manner of sweet concoctions. Mrs Beeton explained how to make the popular chocolate drink in her *Book of Household Management:*

Allow ½ oz. of chocolate to each person; to every oz. allow ½ pint of water, ½ pint of milk. Make the milk and water hot; scrape the chocolate into it, and stir the mixture constantly and quickly until the chocolate is dissolved; bring it to the boiling-point, stir it well, and serve directly with white sugar.

Not one to shy away from sweet concoctions, Isabella Beeton also included 3oz of grated chocolate, along with ½lb of sugar, 1½ pints of cream and six eggs in her rich and blancmange-like recipe for chocolate cream. She used it generously in soufflés, sauces, cakes and as a covering for almonds, pastries and other sweet treats, too.

It is the Quakers, however, who have the strongest ties to the chocolate manufacturing industry. As their passionate pacifist views encouraged hard work and strict ethics regarding the type of commerce they could be involved in, they successfully immersed themselves in food-related businesses. They began as bakers, and are recognised as the first to add chocolate to their cakes. From baking they branched out into making pure chocolate. Joseph Fry is credited with producing the first chocolate bar in 1848, by mixing together cocoa powder and the extracted cocoa butter. It wasn't long before the Quaker Rowntree and Cadbury families were hot on his heels with their own variations; the Cadbury brothers adapting Sir Hans Sloane's recipe to make their own milk chocolate products between 1849 and 1875.

These small enterprises soon grew into highly successful companies employing hundreds of workers across the country. Based in Birmingham, the Cadbury brothers, John and Benjamin, moved their premises outside the restrictive city centre to a new location. Alongside their purpose-built factory, Bourneville, they decided to build a garden village, a small community of well-planned housing and green space – a world away from the slums and harsh conditions suffered in the overcrowded city. By 1895, Cadbury's was a thriving family concern and 140 acres of land were purchased to create their new vision.

The first 143 cottages were built, providing healthy, spacious living conditions for industrious workers. John's third son George explained, 'Why should an industrial area be squalid and depressing? If the country is a good place to live in, why not to work in? No man ought to be condemned to live in a place where a rose cannot grow'. By 1900 the village had increased by a further 313 dwellings, stretching over 330 acres of land. The simple cocoa bean is not only responsible for providing us with one of the world's best loved confectionery products, but it has also been instrumental in creating jobs and better standards of living for thousands of British workers.

Salt & Seasoning

All Victorian cooks were aware that a meal could be spoilt if it was not seasoned correctly. Although salt was used extensively in the preservation of Egyptian mummies, by 2000 BC its preservative qualities had been discovered and were being used to preserve meat, fish and vegetables. Salt rapidly became one of the most important trading commodities in the world, but due to the work needed to extract and transport it, salt was initially an expensive commodity. In Medieval England, salt was kept by wealthy households in a decorative container known as a 'salt'.

Back in the eleventh century, the suffix of 'wich' or 'wych' in the name of an English town was used to denote brine wells or springs in an area. Salt towns in Cheshire, and Droitwich in Worcestershire were even recorded in the Domesday Book, giving a good indication of the significance of salt on the economy. Brine occurred naturally in the abundance of rock salt deposits that lay under the towns in the mid-Cheshire area, and by pumping it from the ground, then boiling it, the salt could be extracted.

Nantwich, Northwich and Middlewich were three of the main salt producing towns that thrived in this region during the nineteenth century. Salt works, brine shafts, new industrial developments and related chemical industries provided work for hundreds of local inhabitants. When the salt mines under Northwich began to collapse, a new source was established further along the River Weaver in Winsford, resulting in the town becoming the largest producer of salt in Britain by 1897.

Much of the success of the Cheshire salt towns can be attributed to their close proximity to the River Weaver and the Trent and Mersey Canal. During the late eighteenth and early nineteenth centuries, these waterways provided an essential highway to ferry the salt to Britain's market towns. By the 1850s the rail network offered a faster, more efficient service. When the Sandbach and Wheelock branch of the North Staffordshire Railway, known as the 'Salt line', opened in 1852 it enabled this important commodity to be transported to industrialised ports, such as Liverpool. This in turn, brought coal to the area to help power the machinery required to process the salt.

For the Victorians, salt was still used as a preservative as well as seasoning. Before the invention of the refrigerator, meat, fish and vegetables were stored in stone jars or containers, layered with salt to prolong their life.

A Taste for a Tipple

The Victorians were just as keen on alcoholic beverages as on their food. Different types of liquor were often thought to reflect a drinker's social standing. For the upper classes, wine would be served during dinner and also, depending upon the occasion, champagne. Sherry was usually viewed as a ladies' drink, whilst after a meal, when the women had withdrawn from the dining room, the gentlemen would take a glass of cognac, or brandy, to accompany their cigars.

During the nineteenth century, whiskey was still seen as an American drink, despite its Scottish origins. Originating from the Caribbean, rum had once been given to sailors as part of their daily rations, but, linked with the working classes, it would not have been the drink of choice for gentlemen. Gin too, was looked upon with derision, as in the past it had been the preferred spirit of the lower end of society. Cheap gin had been easily accessible during the eighteenth century and flowed freely through the brothels and poorer establishments of towns and cities.

Perhaps one of the best portrayals of the social problems caused by gin consumption was depicted in the picture entitled 'Gin Lane' by artist William Hogarth. Designed to be viewed as part of a series alongside 'Beer Street', the two pictures portrayed the evils of drinking gin in contrast to the merits of drinking beer. In an attempt to reduce the consumption of spirits and resulting criminal activity in England, the introduction of the Sale of Spirits Act, commonly known as the Gin Act, was applied to the liquor in 1751, ensuring that it was no longer a cheap tipple.

Tainted by its history, gin was looked down upon by the Victorian upper classes, who linked it with drunkenness, bad behaviour and loose morals. Yet, in the 1820s, London's first 'gin palaces' emerged on the city streets. These establishments were lavishly decorated and fitted out with gas lighting, providing an alluring setting which attracted wealthy men and became a natural haunt for prostitutes. In an article published in *The Evening Chronicle* in 1835, Charles Dickens described how the décor of the gin shops contrasted violently with the surrounding slums of the St Giles area of London:

> The filthy and miserable appearance of this part of London can hardly be imagined by those (and there are many such) who have not witnessed it. Wretched houses with broken windows patched with rags and paper: every room let out to a different family, and in many instances to two or even three – fruit and 'sweet-stuff' manufacturers in the cellars, barbers and red-herring vendors in the front parlours, cobblers in the back ... filth everywhere – a gutter before the houses and a drain behind ...
>
> You turn the corner. What a change! All is light and brilliancy. The hum of many voices issues from that splendid gin-shop which forms the commencement of the two streets opposite; and the gay building with the fantastically ornamented parapet, the illuminated clock, the plate-glass windows surrounded by stucco rosettes, and its profusion of gas-lights in richly-gilt burners, is perfectly dazzling when contrasted with the darkness and dirt we have just left. A bar of French-polished mahogany, elegantly carved, extends the whole width of the place; and there are two side-aisles of great casks, painted green and gold, enclosed within a light brass rail.

From his observations, Dickens admitted that 'gin drinking was a great vice in England' and inextricably linked to poverty. He suggested that the Temperance Societies had better find 'an antidote against hunger, filth, and foul air', than seek to dissuade the poor from drinking. He also warned that, 'until you improve the homes of the poor, or persuade a half-famished wretch not to seek relief in the temporary oblivion of his own misery ... gin-shops will increase in number and splendour'.

Charles Dickens's tales have their fair share of references to alcohol and his characters are depicted enjoying some Victorian favourites with gusto. Scrooge and Bob Cratchit become friends over a bowl of 'Smoking Bishop', a mulled punch made from Seville oranges, spices, red wine and port, and a known favourite of Dickens himself. Attorneys Stryver and Carton enjoy a glass of punch whilst working on a case in the novel *A Tale of Two Cities,* and David Copperfield's good friend Mr Micawber is partial to a gin concoction of his own. In *Martin Chuzzlewit*, there is a description of 'a very large tumbler, piled up to the brim with little blocks of clear transparent ice, through which one or two thin slices of lemon, and a golden liquid of delicious appearance, appealed from the still depths below, to the loving eye of the spectator'. This tempting beverage is revealed as the 'sherry cobbler'.

Dickens also portrayed the consequences for those who became addicted to drink. Krook, a rag and bottle merchant and collector of papers from the novel *Bleak House,* is a regular gin drinker, but his taste for the liquor results in his demise from spontaneous combustion, accelerated by his excessive alcohol consumption. Informed by his observations of the lives of the working classes, Dickens was opposed to the mantra of the Temperance Movement. He believed that everyone deserved the opportunity to have an innocent alcoholic drink, especially the poor, who at times needed something to get through the struggles of their everyday lives. Moderation was the key rather than complete teetotalism.

In the Victorian era, most ordinary families had very little money, their choice of where to spend their income was nearly always governed by the man of the house. Lack of money due to unemployment could see lives spiral out of control, as some men – and women – turned to drink in an attempt to obliterate financial problems and the hardships faced in their difficult lives. In the mid-1800s, temperance campaigners claimed that, 'more was spent every year on drink than on rent'. By the 1870s, the *Illustrated London News* reported that 'people were drinking more than ever – about 10 pints of spirits, 4 pints of wine, and 275 pints of beer each year for every man, woman and child'.

Angus Bethune Reach provided a vivid picture of the beer houses and gin shops of Manchester in an article published in *The Morning Chronicle* in 1849:

> On Saturday night the gin shops are in full feather - their swinging
> doors never hang a moment still ... In a beer-house in Charter Street
> a number of barefooted boys were drinking. The rattle of dominoes
> were heard on every side: the yellow dips which lighted the room

burned with a sickly flicker amid the drafts and the thick tobacco smoke.

This scene was emphasised in George Sims's book, *Horrible London*, published in 1889:

> More than one-fourth of the daily earnings of the citizens of the slums goes over the bars of the public-houses and gin-places. On a Saturday night, butchers, bakers, greengrocers, clothiers, furniture dealers, all the caterers for the wants of the populace, are open till a late hour; there are hundreds of them trading around and about, but the whole lot do not take as much money as three publicans – that is a fact ghastly enough in all conscience. Enter the public-houses, and you will see them crammed. Here are artisans and labourers drinking away the wages that ought to clothe their little ones. Here are the women squandering the money that would purchase food, for the lack of which the children are dying.

Eager to react to such scenes witnessed in towns and cities across Britain, Joseph Livesey spent his life crusading against the evils of drink and the devastation it could cause to individuals and their families. Believing that drinking, even in moderation, only led to drunkenness and addiction, in 1832 Livesey set up the Temperance Movement in Preston, Lancashire, requiring his followers to sign a pledge of total abstinence from alcohol. Livesey's ideals were embraced by several non-conformist churches and paved the way for the development of this mass movement throughout the nineteenth and early twentieth century.

Despite this, alcoholism amongst the poorer classes was still a huge problem. Emmeline Pethick-Lawrence witnessed the effects that alcohol continued to have upon the poor in London, when she took up the role of social worker in 1891. Emmeline later wrote in her book, *My Part in a Changing World*, 'Drunkenness was extremely common … It seemed for many the only refuge from depression and misery'. She added, 'The effect of drunkenness upon the ordinary relationship of husband and wife, parents and children, was disastrous'.

When Liverpool merchant Charles Booth made a detailed study of the labouring classes in London during the 1890s, he sent out investigators to interview people from all walks of life. One vicar in a poor parish revealed:

> A decent man earning 25 shillings a week will give 20 shillings to his wife. She ought to be able to – because in many cases she does – feed

four children, dress herself, and pay the rent out of this. The five shillings left is kept by the man for his beer and tobacco.

At this time, three shillings would buy a quart of milk, 2lbs of bacon, one dozen eggs, and 1lb of cheese.

By the second half of the nineteenth century the Temperance Movement was at its strongest, trying to instil the virtues of abstaining from alcoholic beverages into the working classes and preaching that these lethal concoctions would be the ruin of the nation. But alcohol consumption was a hard habit to break, especially when people had been encouraged to drink alcohol in favour of potentially infected water during the cholera epidemic. Even the political leaders of the time were no strangers to a healthy quantity of alcohol. It was reported William Gladstone, the leader of the Temperance-minded Liberal Party, would occasionally partake of the odd tipple.

In 1854 an outbreak of cholera gave British physician John Snow the opportunity to identify the source of a disease which regularly devastated London's unsanitary and overcrowded streets. By recording the locations of those who died from cholera, he was able to confirm that the infection was spread via contaminated water and finally connected the majority of deaths to the use of one public water pump in Broad Street, Soho. Snow campaigned hard to convince officials that sewage had leaked into the water supply and finally persuaded them to remove the handle of the pump, making it impossible to draw water. As a result, the number of reported cholera cases rapidly decreased, proving Snow's theory that cholera was not spread from person to person but by unsanitary water or food sources.

The introduction of piped, clean drinking water later on in the period would bring about great changes for public health. Once water was safe to drink, the need for daily alcoholic alternatives dwindled.

Ice Cream

Ice cream has become one of our most loved desserts, greatly influenced by the techniques used around the globe, and later by immigrants who brought their culinary secrets with them to Britain. The histories of India, Turkey and other Asiatic countries are littered with references to combinations of fruit juices and sugar poured over snow, then packed into cups to make a refreshing sweet dish. By introducing milk to the ice mixture, the Chinese invented a product which would be recognisable to us today, and Marco Polo is credited with bringing its secrets back to Europe in the early 1300s. Gradually, milk ices, sherbets and ice concoctions became popular in the fashionable eateries of Italy and France. Royal courts served elaborate dishes created from this versatile confection, with King Charles II becoming the first recorded British monarch to experience the delights of ice cream in 1672.

Before refrigeration, a reliable method had to be found to freeze the liquid. A process first documented in the thirteenth century worked by immersing a container of the mixture into a combination of ice and salt, which reacted together to lower the temperature of the ice cream to below freezing point. But the Victorians would make the production of ice cream easy enough for the home cook. By 1853, William Fuller had devised a hand-cranked ice cream-making machine and, teamed with his *Manual Containing Numerous Original Recipes for Preparing Neapolitan Ices*, his invention was widely used by professional caterers, and in the kitchens of the wealthy. It was not until the latter part of the century, that similar machines were made for domestic use, for the housewife becoming more experimental with her menus and eager to mimic the dishes created by the upper classes.

The domestic ice cream-making device was simple in design and consisted of a rotating chamber inserted inside a coppered wooden bucket. The chamber was surrounded by ice and salt to enable the temperature to fall low enough to allow the ingredients within to freeze. A hand crank rotated the chamber so that the contents were evenly cooled.

At this time, an influx of Italian immigrants to the United Kingdom also brought with them the skills and knowledge of some of the best ice cream makers in the world, when they settled in areas such as Manchester and Wales, as well as the capital. Italian vendors would travel the streets with brightly-coloured carts pulled by a pony or pushed by hand, to sell their ice cream from their own pitch, or round. The creamy concoction was served from a 'licking glass' or 'penny lick', which was used as a container then quickly wiped clean ready for the next customer. But when people became aware that this was a health hazard, an alternative had to be found. Paper and metal cones were trialled, with the first edible cones used in the 1890s.

Agnes Marshall recorded these experiments in her book, *Fancy Ices*, published in 1894. With her husband, Agnes had opened the Marshall School of Cookery in Mortimer Street, London a decade earlier, and as well as selling cookery supplies, she was granted a patent for an improved ice cream machine, which enabled a pint of ice cream to be frozen in five minutes.

As the popularity of ice cream continued to grow in Europe, America was developing a taste for it. The first American ice cream parlour opened in New York City in 1776, but it was the introduction of the edible biscuit cone that marked a turning point in the way people all over the world ate their ices. At the 1904 Saint Louis World Fair, ice cream sales were so good during the sweltering heat that George Bang of the Banner Creamery soon ran out of dishes. A nearby stall holder was selling thin wafer waffles, so George came up with the idea of rolling the wafer into a cone and serving the ice cream on top.

By 1923, London saw the first purpose-built ice cream bicycles on their city streets. Cecil Rodd of the ice cream manufacturer Walls developed the motto 'Stop Me and Buy One' and this improved method of transporting their goods saw the business rapidly expand. Numerous Italian cafés began to spring up all over the country, becoming the meeting places for courting couples, who could enjoy each other's company as well as the desserts.

Throughout the nineteenth century, Britain's successful overseas trade brought a plethora of goods to our shores. Passenger travel greatly improved to all areas of the globe and as immigrants arrived in Britain they shared their own culinary knowledge. Scepticism of different and unusual products was gradually overcome and the spread of new exciting dishes enabled us to integrate once 'foreign' ingredients firmly into the British menu.

Chapter Nine

The Professionals

*It is not, in fact, cookery books that we need half so much as cooks
really trained to a knowledge of their duties.*
(Eliza Acton, *Modern Cookery for Private Families*, 1845)

The Victorian culinary world attracted the talents of some of the
most artistic individuals of the age. Chefs became notorious
for ruling their domain with an iron fist, enabling them to produce
innovative fare through dedication and sheer hard work. Although
at the time domestic kitchens were dominated by female cooks, their
male counterparts also had ample opportunities to demonstrate their
culinary skills and many chefs were trained across the Channel.

The restaurant is credited as a French invention established prior to
the Revolution. The term is thought to derive from the word *restaurer*
meaning 'to restore' and described a robust consommé intended to
restore an invalid's strength and vitality. In France, caterers who served
food were known as *traiteurs*, and over the years these two distinct areas
began to merge. Previously, the guilds of *pâtissiers* (pastry chefs) and
charcutiers (butchers specialising in prepared meat products) had all
been licensed by the king. The radical social and political upheaval
caused by the French Revolution brought about the relaxation of such
rigid constraints, allowing anyone to have access to a variety of meals
and foodstuffs if they were able to pay the prices asked. This, in turn,
gave ambitious chefs the opportunity to create dishes for a much wider
market.

Despite male chefs attaining the top jobs in Victorian England and
being heavily influenced by the chefs and styles of the continent, there
was still an acknowledged role for the female cook. French food critic
and journalist Eugène Briffault explained in his 1846 book, *Paris à
Table*:

Those who underestimate the feminine sex where culinary matters
are concerned forget their high level of achievement which has earned
them the accolade of cordon-bleu. It is impossible to bring more skill

and delicacy, more taste and intelligence to the choice and preparation of dishes than women have brought.

Aided by the mechanical innovations of the Industrial Revolution, more changes followed throughout the nineteenth century and mass market foodstuffs began to be produced. As more public eating places were required, jobs within the catering trade saw a rapid increase in roles for both men and women who had an aptitude for and interest in food preparation.

Dressed to Impress

The distinctive chef's uniform of white jacket and tall hat developed out of necessity. The hat, known as a toque, is probably the most recognisable part of the outfit and is said to have been worn by those in the trade as far back as the sixteenth century.

By the 1800s, the term chef (meaning 'chief' in French) was commonly adopted as a title for the professional male cook. The traditional grey worn by French chefs was considered a suitably sombre colour for kitchen apparel, until famed French chef Marie Antoine Carême redesigned the uniform in white to signify cleanliness in the workplace. Made from thick cotton to withstand constant washing, not only did the double-breasted jacket look smart, it also insulated the body against the extreme heat given out by the stoves, acted as protection against splashes from hot liquids and enabled stains to be easily covered. The chef's hat was also reshaped to indicate the different ranks within the kitchen and the chefs wore tall hats, while junior cooks would wear shorter hats or caps.

Celebrity Status

Alexis Benoist Soyer is known as the first 'celebrity chef'. Although born in France, Soyer would become one of the most celebrated cooks in Victorian England. The son of a grocer, he served his apprenticeship in Paris restaurants before becoming the second cook to the French prime minister in 1830. A move to Britain saw Soyer rise to the position of aristocrats' favourite, working for the Duke of Sutherland and the Marquess of Waterford, among other illustrious employers.

But it was during the Irish famine, not sumptuous meals served in upper class dining rooms, when his culinary skills came in to their own. In 1847, he established a soup kitchen in Dublin to serve thousands for free. Whilst there, he wrote a book, *Soyer's Charitable Cookery*, donating the proceeds to the needy, before returning to London to set up a similar soup kitchen operation for the destitute silk weavers of the East End.

In addition to his charitable activities, Soyer became known for his numerous innovations, including using refrigerators cooled by cold water and ovens with adjustable temperatures, even marketing his own 'magic stove', a tabletop cooker allowing people to create food on the move. During the Crimean War, Soyer dispensed advice to the army on cookery techniques and designed his own field stove. He educated soldiers on how to avoid malnutrition and food poisoning, enabling them to prepare an acceptable meal wherever they may find themselves stationed.

But perhaps his most important work was his 1854 book *Shilling Cookery for the People*, aimed at the ordinary householder who wished to create a wholesome meal, without the addition of exotic ingredients or the need for expensive equipment and utensils. Here, Soyer gives hints and tips on how to get the best results from the simplest dishes and describes in detail how to prepare the most basic of fireplaces for cooking a joint of meat:

In the first place, the fire must be made up, and cleared from ashes. Place before it the dripping pan, and from above the fire, suspend from a hook a piece of worsted thread, sufficiently strong to bear the joint, and the hook suspended at the end. Have a piece of stick forked at one end, place against the mantelpiece, so that it keeps the thread at a sufficient distance from the fire. By having two pieces of stick, the distances can be easily managed. Twist the worsted; put on the joint; give it a sufficient distance from the fire. Every cottage should have removable piece of iron, or steel, screwed on the mantelpiece, with teeth fixed in it, so as to be able to hang the joint at any distance from the fire.

By using this method and positioning all meats 18 inches from the fire, Soyer recommends that:

Ten pounds of beef will take from two hours to 2 ½ hours roasting,

Three ribs of beef, boned and rolled, well tied round with paper, will take 2½ hours - only basted once. If beef is very fatty, it does not require basting; if very lean, increase the paper, and baste well.

An eight pound leg of mutton will take 1 ½ hours roasting.

To complete the perfect roasted joint, Soyer advised:

> In roasting of beef, mutton, lamb, pork and poultry, place a dripping pan under the meat, with a little clear dripping or fat, which should be very hot when the meat is basted. A quarter of an hour before serving add half a pint of water to the fat in the dripping; dredge the meat with flour and salt. When the meat is dished up, pour the contents of the pan into a basin, straining it through; remove all the fat, add a little salt to the gravy, and pour it into the dish under the meat.

Good Housekeeping

Professional chefs and kitchen workers cooked for a living but some, like Soyer, saw the advantage of sharing their skills, knowledge and recipes with the masses. From the early 1800s, books and manuals provided advice on all aspects of housewifery and how to run the perfect home, becoming essential, or at least unavoidable, reading for the nineteenth century 'domestic goddess'.

Once, the housewife had relied upon a small notebook in which she would write any useful hints and tips she had picked up from her contemporaries, also using it to record her household accounts and keep all her recipes. When instruction on domestic economy began to find its way into lessons for schoolgirls, specific books dedicated to practical housekeeping were a natural progression and copies could be referred to again and again.

The instructions offered by the growing numbers of household manuals were often lifesavers to the new bride setting up a home or inexperienced servant taking on their first position. Intended as working manuals, they were rarely set in fine bindings, and illustrations were kept to a minimum, although diagrams showing cuts of meat and examples of kitchen equipment seem to have been common.

The Girl's Own Paper

The Girl's Own Paper was a popular publication for young middle-class women during the Victorian era and it reveals a great deal about the type of domestic opinions and subjects deemed to be of most importance to girls at this time. Founded in 1880, the weekly magazine was initially sold for the bargain price of one penny, and promoted, alongside morals and virtues, practical advice to help Victorian women manage their own financial affairs and maintain their homes.

Packed with stories, cookery pages, clothing and needlework tips, history and travel articles, the magazine gave the reader advice on every subject from how to emigrate to the colonies and what to wear to the races to more domestic concerns, like keeping chickens and step-by-step instruction on baking bread. Each issue had at least one cookery segment covering a particular theme, with numerous culinary suggestions and recipe guidance.

An issue published in 1883 contained an article entitled 'Cookery for the Poor', explaining how those with a very tight budget could create nourishing meals economically. The writer took into account the fact that not everyone had the same amount of money to spend, encouraging readers not to judge others less fortunate than themselves. Yet, she still displays obvious snobbery, writing, 'it is the middle class who are, as a rule, willing to receive new ideas, and who are anxious to learn all they can about domestic management' and sweepingly stating that, 'the majority of poor women known little about cookery, and care less'. This snobbery also extends to the daily diets of different classes:

If we go into the poor districts, and notice the food which is offered for sale (for that is the food which is eaten), we see black puddings, small savoury pies, pigs and sheep's heads, liver, hearts, pig's feet, cows heels, tripe, chitterlings, cheap fish, including mussels, whelks and cockles, but we hardly ever see lentils, haricot beans or maize; yet district visitors and charitable people have tried their best to make lentils popular – and, so far, without success.

Rather condescendingly, the writer adds:

there are a great many clever managing women amongst the poor who cook very well, and who are willing to prepare good food for their families. All honour to these virtuous ones! They are doing their life's work nobly, and they will have their reward in seeing their children grow up healthy, and knowing that their husbands are steady and respectable.

It would have been difficult enough for poor working class housewives to make ends meet without the scornful opinions of the middle class women, who thought they could run a home much more efficiently in similar circumstances. It was very easy to come up with a range of dishes when you had access to the wide variety of ingredients a larger family budget could afford.

Along with the subject of food, came the moral question of drink, and the article advised when an alcoholic beverage should be consumed and its possible effects, not only upon the appetite but also on the lifestyle of the drinker. Apparently, the answer to overindulgence lay in beef tea:

> A large number of those who 'take to drinking' begin to go wrong by taking beer as a substitute for food. They feel exhausted, there is no food 'handy' , and so they take a draft of beer and this quickly revives them, the experience is repeated, they gradually acquire the habit of relying on beer, and go from bad to worse. If some true friend had given them a cupful of good beef tea, or a cupful of coffee to drink instead of the beer, they would have felt better almost as quickly and no harm would have been done. Unfortunately, however, beer is always to be had, and beef tea is a rarity, and so the mischief is done.

What the Dickens!

Charles Dickens may have been adept at describing the favourite dishes of his fictional characters but he was not the only one in his family whose love of food found its way into their written work. His wife Catherine (née Hogarth) was just as accomplished at putting pen to paper when it came to her passion for cookery. Despite raising ten children, Catherine found time to host regular dinner parties at their London home, the menus bursting with dishes to satisfy the appetites of the most distinguished guests.

Her decision to collate her most popular recipes and share them with the public resulted in the colourfully titled *What Shall We Have for Dinner?*, which had an equally descriptive subtitle of 'Satisfactorily Answered by Numerous Bills of Fare for from Two to Eighteen Persons'. Her love of dinner parties ensured that the book included a wide range of recipes suitable to grace the dinner table on any occasion, with 'leg of mutton stuffed with oysters' being just one example.

Under the pseudonym of 'Lady Maria Clutterbuck', the book was published in 1851 and it sheds light on the dining habits of the middle class Victorian. Course after course of soup and light fish dishes followed by meaty mains, a choice of desserts and a cheese board, were what the average dinner guest could expect. One summer menu features 'Oxtail Soup, Salmon in Lobster Sauce, Mackerel a la Maitre d'Hotel, Boiled Spring Chicken and Asparagus Sauce, Lobster Curry, Sweetbreads, Veal Olives, a Fore Quarter of Lamb, Oyster Patties and Ducklings accompanied by peas, new potatoes and asparagus'. If that wasn't enough a choice of dessert was recommended of 'Currant and Raspberry Tart with Cold Custard' or 'Lemon Jelly and Charlotte Russe'. This was a fine spread for a party of between eight to ten people.

Some of her recipes were complex, with an extensive list of ingredients and various stages of preparation, even for something as relatively simple as asparagus soup. But there was a good mix of inexpensive, nourishing meals thrown in too. In this small volume, Catherine displays elements of thrift alongside extravagance, but with a distinct lack of vegetables. She undoubtedly catered for those with a love of cookery whether for a large gathering or a small family meal.

From stewed eel to stuffed haddock, this manual was extremely popular, prompting reprints in 1852 and 1854.

Mrs Isabella Beeton

Today the most well-known Victorian domestic guide is, of course, *Mrs Beeton's Book of Household Management*. At the age of 21, Isabella Beeton began to write a column for her publisher husband's periodical, *The English Woman's Domestic Magazine*. Such was the interest shown in her advice that she went on to write her own manual, *Mrs Beeton's Book of Household Management*, initially issued in 1859 as a series of 33 monthly instalments, before it was released as a single volume in 1861. Selling 60,000 copies in its first year, the book inspired readers to try out new recipes and follow practical tips on how to successfully run their homes, putting emphasis on the woman being in charge of her own domain.

Even Isabella Beeton's opening sentences instil confidence in the home cook:

> As with the commander of an army, or the leader of any enterprise, so as it is with the mistress of the house. Her spirit will be seen through the whole establishment; and just in proportion as she performs duties intelligently and thoroughly, so will her domestics follow in her path.

Mrs Beeton subtly implied that the skills required to run a successful home gave power and authority to the middle class female. For women who had spent a lifetime under the influence of their menfolk, her words inspired self-belief through accomplishment and it was no wonder that this book became hugely popular. Perhaps more than anything, it assured readers and aided them in every possible cookery and household problem. The depth of content enabled good home-cooked fare to be produced on a daily basis by providing lists of ingredients, information on the duration of the cooking process and the price of the finished meal, allowing different dishes to be considered within the confines of a household budget.

Sadly, Mrs Beeton did not live to see the fruits of her labour. Five years after she began her culinary tome, Isabella died at the age of 28 from puerperal fever, only eight days after giving birth for the fourth time. Despite her early demise, she lived on through her published work to become a household name, with sales of her book reaching two million copies within three years of her death.

Mrs Beeton's success followed in the wake of and overtook contemporaries, such as Eliza Acton whose 1855 book *Modern Cookery for Private Families* was aimed at middle class women who were overseeing the running of the kitchen and planning their own meals. Acton's emphasis was on easy to prepare dishes requiring the minimum of ingredients. Similarly, *The Modern Cook*, published in 1846 by Charles Francatelli, was so popular that it went through 29 editions. Francatelli catered for those who wanted slightly more advanced cookery techniques, yet to remain economical with ingredients.

Encouraged by Isabella Beeton's success, there was a flurry of publications. By 1887, Jane Ellen Panton, a journalist and author on domestic issues, completed her book *From Kitchen to Garret* aimed at young householders setting up their first home. Mary Eliza Haweis produced a selection of titles on the domestic layout of the home, while in her 1899 book *The Hostess of Today*, Linda Larned gave assistance on 'selecting a menu suitable for the most elaborate repast or the simplest meal ... estimating the cost of it at average market prices'.

Mrs Beeton's work, however, rather than that of her competitors, has left its mark in the culinary hall of fame. Her observations show the sheer variety of food available to the Victorians. She lists 45 types of fish, their cost per pound and the months in which they were in season; pages of 'provisions and household requisites'; a list of store cupboard favourites including 'Calves Foot Jelly', 'Pickled Mangoes' and 'Fine Mushroom Ketchup'; as well as an illustrated display of cordials and essences for every occasion.

She pointed out the importance of tinned goods, emphasising that they 'now occupy an important place in our food supply, being available at any time, and handy substitutes when fresh provisions may be difficult to procure'. She also reveals possible shortcuts for housewives, explaining that 'Finest Potted Shrimp, Potted Tongue and Boiled Beef' were essential for sandwich making, and that tinned oysters provided a great 'standby' for fine dining.

A Cook's Own Book

Although working cooks were usually highly experienced in their field, many compiled simple journals of their favourite recipes or new techniques they had discovered. During the 1880s, Avis Crocombe was the resident cook at Audley End in Essex – one of the finest Jacobean houses in England. Her recipe book is priceless for the social historian, as she has included details of her career, written in pencil on the front page:

> Avis Crocombe – was cook / housekeeper to Sir Thomas and Lady Beauchamp, Langley Park, Norfolk 1870 – 1873 ... and ... Cook – housekeeper to Lord and Lady Braybrook, Audley End, Saffron Walden.

From simple sponge biscuits and gingerbread cake to elder wine and almond faggots, Avis recorded all of her favourite recipes in her spiky Victorian hand. One in particular that stands out as a dish perfect for a hot summer day is her 'Cucumber Ice Cream', which requires a combination of one peeled and deseeded cucumber simmered in a pan with 4oz sugar, a pinch of salt, and ½ pint of water. This would then have been sieved before blending in one pint of double cream and one or two small glasses of ginger wine. A few drops of green food colouring were added to the final mix to enhance the overall look of this refreshing, if slightly unusual dessert.

Practising Thrift

In Victorian Britain the phrase 'Waste Not Want Not' was taken extremely seriously. It appeared on decorative pottery, with the wording giving an appropriately moral touch to the design. In the kitchens of

Erddig Hall near Wrexham, the phrase was elaborately painted on the wall above the range, to reinforce the mantra to the domestic staff and shows that thrift was also required in wealthy mansions, not merely in ordinary homes.

In an effort to make leftovers stretch further, small pieces of meat were used in appetising *entrées*, the bones and trimmings providing an essential base for stocks and soups. Cubes of fat were rendered down to reuse for frying, whilst leftover sweet dishes were decorated to make them look even more delicious on their second serving.

Whether in working class or wealthy homes, one of the commonest causes of waste in the kitchen was stale bread. Once hard, dry and ostensibly tasteless, there were many times when there was no option but to relegate it to the bin. Writing in 1883, cook Phyllis Brown declared that 'servants will not eat it, beggars will not accept it as a gift and puddings have been made of it so persistently that families unite in declining to partake of bread-and-butter pudding'. She makes it her mission to explain some interesting ways to breathe new life into bread that was past its best, including:

> Broken bread is excellent for thickening purées and sauces. The bread should be stewed with the flavouring vegetables, then rubbed through a sieve with them. If it is toasted before being put into the liquor, it will help impart colour as well as the consistency of the purée.

Phyllis's list of thrifty ideas was endless, ranging from various sweet puddings such as apple charlotte and a Viennese pudding made with eggs, candied peel, sultanas, milk and sugar, which she explained, despite having no flour or suet in the mixture 'tastes very much like a rich plum pudding', to simple toasted brown breadcrumb crusts to serve with game, and 'sippets' (croutons) to add to soup.

One not very enticing idea was to make 'Toast and Water' by:

> cutting the bread very thin, and toasting it slowly till it is very crisp and dry throughout, and of a dark brown colour. Plunge it into a jug of water, let it stand for about half an hour and then decant it into a water bottle. The liquor should be as clean and bright as Sherry.

Another less than palatable recipe called 'Bread Raspings with Cold Milk' required the cook to:

Warm stale bread in the oven till dry and lightly browned. Crush it roughly with a rolling pin, put the crumbs into a bowl, and pour over them cold milk, which has been beaten up with the white of egg and if permitted a tablespoonful of brandy.

Phyllis then adds a hint for its use, 'I have been told that this preparation is valuable in cases of diarrhoea'.

Labour-saving Devices

Cooking on a kitchen range was hard work and required raking out the ashes each morning and applying a coat of black lead at least once a week. Those with a range were much more fortunate than the poorer classes, who still cooked over an open grate, but easier options had to be found. By the mid-1800s, kitchen ranges began to change dramatically and the graft involved in both using and cleaning them was reduced, greatly improving the everyday life of the cook and kitchen staff. The first temperature controlled ovens were complicated devices with a whole system of flues and plates, but there was real excitement at the prospect of being able to regulate the heat.

Like many other new and innovative creations, a glimpse of what the future might hold for Victorian cooks was witnessed at the Great Exhibition of 1851, when early versions of gas-powered devices were showcased. Although much more practical, the public were at first sceptical about the use of gas in their homes and the risk that a gas explosion might occur at their property. Consequently, gas ovens only caught on with the general public near the end of the Victorian era.

As the century progressed, an array of gadgets and time-saving devices began to accumulate within the Victorian kitchen. Knife polishers, free-standing roasters and butter churns were just some of the equipment required to speed up activities below stairs. According to the *Oxford English Dictionary*, the first recorded entry of the term 'kitchen gadget' is said to have appeared in the 1951 edition of the *Good Housekeeping Home Encyclopaedia*, but newfangled utensils were actually appearing on the culinary scene much earlier than that.

The Victorians loved nothing better than a kitchen appliance designed for a specific task, which ultimately made the job easier. After their initial scepticism, most were eager to try out new labour-saving devices, including apple peelers, cherry pitters, cheese graters and later, can openers. In an era of innovation, the kitchen did not escape the nineteenth century inventor's eager eye and, although some designs were novelty items soon to be relegated to the back of a drawer, most cooks embraced new ideas with open arms.

Other gadgets helped to free up members of the kitchen staff. The fireplace provided an open space to roast large joints of meat. To enable the spit on which the joint was placed to turn slowly over the heat, without requiring the cook to rotate it constantly, the spit was attached to a jack. This gadget saw many changes over the years, as budding engineers tried to perfect their designs. Originally, animals were used to pull the mechanism around, but by the nineteenth century, a system of weights and pulleys provided movement, and an alternative option was to harness the rising air in smoke drawn up the chimney, to power the jack. For smaller pieces of meat, a meat mangle or tenderiser allowed the kitchen maid to take out her aggression in the name of food preparation, whilst the sausage stuffer with a wooden plunger and metal spout helped to speed up the job of creating the 'breakfast banger'.

Hand-held toasting forks were used to spear bread and brown it over the flames to make toast, but this technique soon developed into hinged devices mounted on the hearth side, which could hold the bread yet enabled it to be turned to toast both sides with very little human intervention. Pot hooks and rods of varying lengths were used to hold the pans over the fire, but also enabled each pan to be moved into, or out of, the heat, helping to regulate the temperature of the food being cooked. This arrangement allowed the cook to choose whether to boil or simmer her ingredients. At any one time, the hearth might also be home to a kettle for rendering fat, a flat griddle pan for making crumpets, pikelets and pancakes, and a cast iron coffee bean roaster, with a handle to rotate the contents, preventing the beans from burning.

The Victorians loved order, symmetry, precise design and regimented layouts even in their vegetables, with bean cutters and asparagus bunchers to create a uniform size. Mrs Beeton would have approved. Although she didn't refer to them as gadgets, her *Book of Household Management* had stressed the importance of kitchen tools back in 1861. She listed no less than 37 essential utensils for the art of cookery. Among the equipment she advised cooks to purchase was a pestle and mortar to crush ingredients to a powder or paste, along with grinders, choppers, mashers and squeezers.

Before the introduction of plastic containers, stoneware, earthenware, and later, glass, were used to house groceries, which were often sold unwrapped. Wood and tin boxes were common choices to keep dry goods moisture-free. In fact, many kitchen items were made from wood, usually oak, as it was considered hard-wearing and could be easily cleaned using boiling hot water. The only drawback was that it sometimes became discoloured. Wooden spoons would have been used every day and had a hole in the handle so they could be hung on a hook, or stored together in a ceramic jar in a prominent position. They were always preferred to metal spoons, which could sometimes taint the flavour of certain food items.

Teaching, Training and Tuition

When the Elementary Education Act was introduced in 1870, it offered free primary education for children throughout England and Wales for the first time. Prior to this, only those with the means to pay for tuition were able to provide schooling for their children. The Education Act also gave school boards the power to build and run the establishments, and to compel children aged between five and thirteen to attend. This was a huge benefit to the children of the poor, who had previously gone out to work from an early age and contributed to the household income. Although the family would lose this money, the youngsters were now entitled to an education, with the expectation of better future prospects.

Within ten years the scheme was a success and, as the routine was instilled, the curriculum developed. In *The Modern Cook* (1846), chef Charles Elmé Francatelli described his conviction that, 'The palate is as capable and nearly as worthy of education as the eye and ear'. The education boards also believed in teaching children basic cooking skills and girls were taught needlework and cookery. The latter enabled them not only to prepare a meal for the family table, but also provided them with the proficiency to find work in catering or domestic service. Larger schools even had a cookery classroom built purely for this purpose, with a demonstration area to allow the teacher to instruct her pupils. The preparation table, gas stove and range enabled the dishes to be created by following written instructions off the blackboard. The pupils enjoyed putting their new-found knowledge into practice at home.

By the late 1880s, with a background as a fully certified cook and the ability and flair to instruct others on the intricacies of kitchen work, the teacher could expect to earn between £80 and £100 a year. As well as preparing the lessons, her role would include ordering all the products for the dishes she planned to demonstrate, keeping good accounts and the stockroom in order.

Mrs Beeton and Eliza Acton had planted the seed of an idea that it was good for women to gain knowledge and increase their culinary skills. Towards the latter end of the century and well into the Edwardian era, dedicated cookery schools for middle class young ladies began to appear. They encouraged a new breed of young women to look beyond the recipes they were used to and begin experimenting for themselves in preparation for running their own households. Instead of simply employing staff, they would have more idea of the skills needed and an understanding of food preparation. This ultimately gave them a feeling of control in their own homes.

The man might still have been the master of the house, but the Victorian woman was mistress of the kitchen!

Chapter Ten

The Country House Garden

The onion and its satin wrappings is among the most beautiful of vegetables and is the only one that represents the essence of things. It can be said to have a soul.

(Charles Dudley Warner, *My Summer in a Garden*, 1871)

Most nineteenth century country estates were equipped with a kitchen garden, a greenhouse to grow exotic fruit, and an ice house to store ice. The kitchen or walled garden was manned by a team of professional, knowledgeable staff, who supplied the house with fresh produce and flowers and foliage for the indoor floral and table displays.

The garden design usually consisted of a structured layout, incorporating geometric patterns to segregate various types of produce. Vital to the culinary requirements of the house, it was also visually appealing with year-round interest provided by perennials and evergreen shrubs. Known in France as a *potager*, this style of layout developed from the French Renaissance garden, where edible and inedible plants grew side-by-side requiring minimum maintenance. With a combination of low-lying bushes and shrubs, taller plants and flowers offered height and drew attention to the garden display.

Pleasing to the eye as well as functional, small box hedges separated crops and herbs, with vegetables planted in rows. Despite this formality, there was also a carefree, softer look to the garden, due to the combination of varieties planted. The south-facing wall caught most of the sun and was used to grow peaches, plums, cherries and tomatoes. Figs, pears and apples would thrive on the west-facing wall, arranged in styles known as *espalier* – grown flat against the wall and supported by a lattice frame. These were constructed in fan shapes for stoned fruit, or in cordons to grow fruit in smaller areas and for varieties that could bear fruit on short side shoots.

A dedicated team of gardeners working long hours, year-round, in all weathers ensured that the garden always looks its best and produced the maximum amount of fruit and vegetables on an allotted piece of land. Facilities like potting sheds, storehouses and boiler rooms were often built to utilise the back walls of the kitchen gardens and, in some cases, served as the basis for one wall of the gardener's cottage. Based close by, employees were always available and could act as night watchmen.

At Rode Hall in Cheshire, the cottage built on the south-facing wall of the kitchen garden was occupied by Head Gardener, John Bailey. From here he was able to oversee the plants in his care, as well as keeping a watchful eye on the garden boys who lived in the bothy opposite. The boys were required to carry out a variety of menial, yet essential, jobs including stoking the chimneys in the wall which supported the espalier trees, helping to protect the fruit trees against the cold and enabling certain varieties to be grown all year round.

At Audley End House in Saffron Walden, Essex, young gardener William Cresswell kept a detailed diary throughout 1874 recording his daily tasks, the types of produce grown, and the effects of the weather upon the crops. On 27 July he noted, 'Wind SE beautiful day. Cleaned up orchard house. Greenhouse and part of stove whitewashed to afford shading to plants inside. Earthed up beans in third vinery which were planted on the 13th'.

The walled garden at Audley End House was originally located quite close to the main house, but was later moved to incorporate an orchard and expand the growing area. A vegetable garden situated close to the kitchens enabled fresh supplies to be delivered to the cook at a moment's notice, though due to the layout of the estate this was not always possible. At Harewood House in West Yorkshire, the walled garden was a 20-minute walk through the grounds from the kitchen, whilst at Shugborough Hall in Staffordshire, a new walled garden built to feed the household during the Victorian era was situated half a mile from the mansion.

There are two schools of thought regarding Victorian walled gardens. The first was that the addition of walls would protect vegetables from the elements, but in reality only an extremely high construction could do this successfully. Some gardens were simply so big that any wall would have had little effect against a howling gale. The second was that the walls were needed to protect the crops from theft. Kitchen gardens contained vast amounts of expensive produce – an appealing prospect for a hungry villager struggling to feed his family. 'I was not short of work as there was always something going wrong', explained parkman and night watchman, William Lowe, who worked at Hardwick Hall between 1884 and 1939, 'but it was my motto to do my best for my employer and the patrons of the park'.

The size of the garden, and the scale and diversity of produce raised, grew in direct proportion to the owner's wealth and need to feed both their family and household staff. Between Queen Victoria's ascent to the throne and the start of the First World War, Britain saw great changes. The Empire was expanding, trade was thriving, new inventions and industrial developments benefited many entrepreneurs. Businessmen and their families needed homes reflecting their wealth in which to entertain influential society friends. The size, style and facilities of their home were all calculated to make a good impression with their contemporaries, as it was a platform to showcase their prosperity and affluence.

Team Work: The Cook and Gardener

The relationship between the country house head gardener and the cook was necessarily one of mutual respect – one could not really survive in their role without the support of the other. The cook relied upon the gardener to bring her the best seasonal produce, and the cook's culinary know-how guided the gardener and helped him to anticipate the amount of each crop he would be expected to grow for the table.

The kitchen garden was a working garden and not just a show garden for the house. The cook's choice of recipes and the gardener's ability to successfully cultivate the ingredients reflected on the family and their ability to entertain and provide a varied and fashionable menu for their guests. Every gardener had his own tips and tricks passed on to him during his apprenticeship by a father, grandfather or colleague. He, in turn, would pass these ideas on to his own apprentices or sons, keeping the traditions alive.

As the most senior member of the outdoor staff, the head gardener would usually live with his family in a cottage on his employer's estate. In 1883, when Maria Medley commissioned the walled gardens on her Winsford Towers Estate in Devon, she employed 31 garden staff. Maria's head gardener was paid a salary of £100 a year. The size of the estate determined the amount of garden staff; some would be permanent staff and apprentices, whilst others were seasonal labourers and might be laid off during the winter months. No matter what the weather, the head gardener at Winsford Towers, like many other estates, was responsible for a constant, year-long supply of fresh produce for the table. This was supplied not only at the Devon estate but also parcelled up and sent by train to Paddington Station in London, for delivery to the kitchens of Maria's home in Park Lane.

Beer on Tap

Keen to document the history of the family and everyday life at Chatsworth House in Derbyshire, the 6th Duke of Devonshire, William George Spencer Cavendish, kept a journal. Published and privately printed in 1844, it was entitled the *Handbook of Chatsworth and Hardwick*. Writing in the first person, the Duke included a huge amount of information and even included a reference to 'the twelve Apostles', the large oak casks carved with the arms of the first Duke and designed to store beer which resided in the cellars of Chatsworth.

The estate brewed its own beer above the stable block, and used an underground pipe installed by the 6th Duke, documented in his journal as '1059 feet long', which carried the amber liquid directly to the house. It was not until the twentieth century that a tap was discovered inserted into the pipe near the rose garden. It seems that the gardeners had found a cunning way to siphon off the beer and enjoy a secret tipple, unbeknownst to their employer. In recognition of their ingenuity, a brand of beer available in the Chatsworth shop today has been named 'Gardener's Tap' in their honour.

A Blossoming Romance

When Hannah Gregory accepted the coveted position of housekeeper on the extensive Chatsworth estate, it was a role she would dedicate her life to. As the Duke noted in the *Handbook of Chatsworth and Hardwick*, Hannah Gregory was 'the housekeeper who dwelt here for half a century'. Working for the 6th Duke of Devonshire would have earned her respect both within the community and her own family.

Along with overseeing all household duties and female staff, working in conjunction with the cook and meeting the daily requests of the Devonshire family, Hannah would also unwittingly become a matchmaker. Whilst taking breakfast with her niece Sarah Bown the estate's new head gardener, Joseph Paxton, arrived. Hannah introduced the pair and for both parties it was love at first sight. Within nine months the couple were married and took up residence in the gardener's cottage on the estate. By the time of the 1841 census they had four children, and whilst Hannah continued in her position as housekeeper, Sarah supported her husband in his rapidly blossoming career. Joseph Paxton went on to become one of the Victorian era's most famous garden designers, architects and visionaries.

Although Paxton's work took him further afield – for example, during the construction of Crystal Palace in London in preparation for the Great Exhibition of 1851 – Chatsworth was his true home. When Hannah left service and later passed away, she was replaced by Elizabeth Bicknell, who had previously been a barmaid in Buxton. Loyal to her aunt and her faultless housekeeping regime, Sarah explained that during the Duke's absence, the 'upstart' Bicknell had been reportedly eating off the silver and entertaining her friends at the Duke's expense. This caused much furore before Elizabeth Bicknell was replaced with the much more suitable Mrs Hastie, who ran the house in the same manner as her dependable predecessor.

Paxton died at the age of 64 and the couple were buried together in a large tomb in St Peter's churchyard at Edensor, the village on the estate he had helped to create.

Tools for the Task

As nineteenth century Britain's love of gardening snowballed, magazines, periodicals and dedicated journals explained the intricacies of plant cultivation, offered advice and recommended the latest gardening gadgets, whilst plant nurseries and seed specialists suggested new and exciting varieties. Tool manufacturers promoted catalogues to show their latest wares; some newfangled devices didn't last a season, whilst others were developed over the decades, their designs standing the test of time and still in use today.

A vast knowledge of horticulture was crucial to the professional gardener, but he also needed the correct tools to get the most from the plants in his care. He would purchase the best tools that his budget would allow, in the hope that many of them would last a lifetime. The tool sheds would be packed with implements, with a small area set aside to maintain them on the premises. A fork and trowel were essential for aerating the soil, lifting compost, digging out weeds and preparing holes for planting. Secateurs were needed for pruning, clipping and dead-heading, whilst a small hoe enabled weeding to be carried out in-between established plants.

But the simplest devices were used time and time again. For example, to collect honey from the beehives without being stung, a bee smoker was required. A small piece of rag was added to the cylinder at the bottom of the hand-held device and lit. By squeezing the leather pump, the smoke could be directed through the conical nozzle and into the hive, which had the effect of making the bees sleepy, allowing the honey to be collected without angering them. Similarly, a wooden tool – very much like the rattles used at football matches – was swung around rapidly to make a noise and scare the birds away from the vegetable garden. Young boys were often employed on estate gardens from an early age and this would have been one of their jobs.

Compost Bins

Ensuring that the soil was as well nourished as possible meant that regular fertilising was essential. Compost bins were set up to recycle any useful garden waste and topped up with manure collected from the animals on the estate. Lids were placed on the bins so that they did not become waterlogged in winter, but this had the dual purpose of creating a warm atmosphere which would help to break down the contents within.

The ability to grow large amounts of produce inevitably resulted in times when there was too much stock to be used in the kitchen at once. Fruit stores were set up to house the excess fruit until it was needed. Well ventilated and protected with fly screens to minimise pest damage, and kept dark to deter the fruit from ripening, it could still be an extremely difficult job to ensure the long-term storage of such perishable produce. Any gardener who could master this, allowing his employer to have exotic varieties of fruit served at his dining table, was worth his weight in gold.

Pest Control

Pests like rabbits and birds were a constant problem for Victorian gardeners, but natural preventative measures and techniques were employed to minimise their impact. Domed wicker or willow covers were used to shield some of those vegetables particularly enjoyed by the rabbits – allowing through light and air but keeping the rabbits out. They were easily manoeuvrable and could be swapped to areas of the garden which needed the most protection.

To try and alleviate pest damage, traditional techniques of sowing plants that pests did not like next to their favourite crops went some way to prevent spoilage long before commercially developed sprays and repellents were readily available. Pesticides used at this time were often untested – it was not unusual for a gardener to spray his plants with arsenic, not realising the need to wear a mask.

A Herbal History

Depending upon the dimensions of the kitchen garden, herbs were either incorporated within the plan or given a specific area of their own where they could flourish naturally. Some were clipped into an attractive shape – a popular practice in the traditional Knot Garden. The herbs the gardener chose to cultivate would provide background foliage and an aromatic scent, whilst their quick growth ensured a constant supply of seasoning to enhance the flavour of dishes in the kitchen.

From beauty aids to disinfectants, herbs have been used for thousands of years. The Romans used mint and other varieties in their dishes to disguise the taste of old meat. Flower heads were scattered in bath water in the belief that bathing would help keep disease away. The Romans are credited with developing the first formal herb gardens and later, medieval monks continued to develop their uses in their infirmaries, passing remedies on to travellers and pilgrims establishing a barter and trade system.

By the sixteenth century, travellers returned to Britain with exotic species from America and the Far East, which were subsequently grown for both medicinal and culinary use. From their overseas discoveries, two herbalists published their works: John Gerard in 1593 and, most famously, Nicholas Culpepper in 1660. Culpepper was a trained London apothecary and made the growing of herbs fashionable in Elizabethan England, with elaborate herb gardens established at grand houses, such as Buckfast Abbey in Devon and Bolton Castle in Yorkshire. His book *Culpepper's Herbal* is still in use today.

Preparing the Ground for Herbs

When planning a herb garden, first the gardener would decide on a suitable location in full sunlight. Most herbs thrive in a well-drained area, which is sunny for most of the day but sheltered from the elements. In autumn or early spring, the gardeners would prepare the ground, by breaking up any large sods of earth and raking it to a medium texture. Digging in plenty of home-made compost or manure would feed the plants throughout the season, helping the soil to keep its structure and allow good drainage. The success of the crop was dependent upon the type of soil used, so modification was often needed to provide the best growing conditions.

Sandy Soil – feels rough to the touch, very gritty and is prone to over-drainage in summer, resulting in lost nutrients. By adding organic matter it can be made easier to cultivate, although care must be taken in winter when excess moisture can lead to rotting.

Chalky Soil – this alkaline soil can contain lots of stones, which make it dry out in summer. Due to this, nutrients are lost resulting in the poor growth of herbs and yellowing leaves. Digging in plenty of fertiliser when preparing the ground can help to combat this.

Clay Soil – is one of the worst types of soil to work, as it is wet and soggy in winter and very hard in summer, but also the best soil for growing just about anything.

Silty Soil – nutritious and fertile, it contains minerals and organic particles. When dry, it has the texture of dark sand but holds its moisture and is pliable to work with.

Peaty Soil – its spongy texture can retain too much water, so often needs artificial drainage – a fine layer of crushed stone combats this.

Loamy Soil – usually made up of sand, silt and clay, this soil is easily worked and quite densely packed. It is rich in nutrients and moisture but does drain well allowing sufficient air to reach the roots of the plants.

Victorian gardeners knew the land they worked like the back of their hands, but would teach their apprentices the principles for establishing the soil type they had to work with, as they might move around the country during their career. After watering the chosen area and examining the results they could determine that:

- Water disappears quickly on sandy or gravel soil.
- Water remains on clay.
- By picking up a handful of soil and gently squeezing:
- Clay soil stays in a lump.
- Sandy or gravel soil falls apart.
- Peat has a spongy feel.
- Loam and silt hold their shape but not as rigidly as clay or as crumbly as sand.

Herbs and Their Uses

PLANT	DESCRIPTION	USES (Cooking)	USES (Medicinal)
Angelica *Angelica archangelica*	Aromatic plant which can grow up to two metres high. Likes to grow in partial shade in rich, light soil.	Can be candied for cake decoration.	Once burned as incense to ward off pestilence and the plague.
Basil *Ocimum basillicum*	Perennial. Intense smell and flavour. Leaves bruise easily.	Italian dishes, soups, salads.	
Bay *Laurus nobilis*	Evergreen. Dislikes cold wind.	Leaves can easily be dried for use in soups and stews.	Used by the Ancient Romans and Greeks to crown their heroes.
Borage *Borago officinalis*	Hardy Annual. Blue flowers with hairy leaves.	Traditionally used in a final drink for those who were off to the Crusades – said to bring courage.	Said to relieve melancholy.
Caraway *Carum carvii*	White flowered plant with feather foliage which tastes like parsley.	Seeds used for flavouring liqueurs and their aromatic flavour makes them good in soups, stews and on salads.	Traditionally, placing caraway between a person's clothes was said to deter thieves.
Catmint *Nepeta cataria*	Perennial. Can be grown successfully from seed and has a fragrance of mint and lemon. Said to keep rats away but can attract cats if not protected.	Herbal tea can be made from the leaves.	Can be used to dye textiles and wool.
Chamomile *Chamaemelum nobile*	Annual. Pale cream flowers. Grown in lawns and borders due to its fragrant smell.	Used in herbal tea.	Chamomile tea is a headache, stress reliever and aids digestion.
Chives *Allium tuberosum*	Perennial. Mild garlic flavour. Grow easily in or outdoors. Can be planted to ward off carrot fly and aphids.	Chop for use in salads, soups or as a garnish.	
Coriander *Coriandrum sativum*	Annual. Both delicate green foliage and seeds can be used. Fresh smell and flavour.	Used in Asian cooking – soups, stews and stir fries.	Said to deter fevers.

Herb	Description	Culinary use	Medicinal use
Cumin *Cuminum cyminum*	A delicate plant which requires a sheltered spot to achieve the best results.	Seeds are used in curries and pickles and to flavour bread and cakes.	
Hyssop *Hyssopus officinalis*	Hardy Perennial. Flowers in blue or pink attracts bees.	Used to add flavour to stewed fruit.	A tea made from Hyssop was used to treat coughs and colds.
Lemon Balm *Melissa officinalis*	Perennial. Aromatic lemon scent.	Once used to make a refreshing herbal tea.	Used to treat colds and fevers.
Marjoram *Origanum majorana*	Perennial. High tolerance to damp.		Comforts the stomach.
Mint All types	Rampant plant – try to contain in a pot.	Mint sauce with lamb.	Mouthwash, stomach ailments, wounds.
Rosemary *Rosmarinus officinalis*	Perennial. Spiky, pine like leaves. Robust flavour.	Used to flavour meat.	Leaves boiled in white wine said to make a stringent face wash.
Rue *Ruta graveolens*	Perennial. Rounded leaves, bitter smell.	Considered unsafe for human use by modern practitioners.	Once used as a holy water sprinkler.
Sage *Salvia officinalis*	Perennial. Powerful flavour.	Used in stuffings and to flavour meat.	Can be used as an antiseptic.
Tarragon *Artemisia dracunculus*	Prefers warm, dry conditions.	Used in white wine vinegar to produce tarragon vinegar.	
Thyme *Thymus vulgaris*	Perennial. Tiny leaves. Prefers well drained soil. If grown in a pot can be used all year round.	Used in bouquet garni and to flavour meat stews.	Used as an astringent.

Greenhouses and Hothouses

Before 1851, British residents of properties with six or more windows were liable to pay window tax. This was calculated on weight, not the size of the panes, so the glass was often made deliberately thin to try to alleviate the cost. In some cases, people used to brick up one of their windows to reduce the amount of money they would be required to pay, whilst the rich flaunted their wealth by having even larger windows installed in their mansions and country homes.

Naturally, when the tax was abolished the use of glass became more prevalent. Three years previously, in 1848, plate glass had been invented, making glass far more affordable. Joseph Paxton demonstrated the enormous possibilities of glass constructions when he was commissioned to build London's enormous Crystal Palace for the Great Exhibition in 1851. His previous experience in building an iron-framed conservatory at Chatsworth House earned him the backing and support of his contemporaries. Covering three quarters of an acre, at the time the tent-like structure was the largest glass building in the world. Paxton used this as a model for the far larger Crystal Palace, a mammoth construction covering 19 acres – higher than Westminster Abbey, and five times as long as the Palm House in Kew Gardens. It took the builders 22 weeks of backbreaking work to erect the structure, with its 293,635 panes of glass.

The revelation of the endless possibilities that glass constructions offered, saw large greenhouses gracing wealthy estates. The builders harnessed the sun's rays to their full potential by erecting them on the south-facing walls of the kitchen gardens. But Victorian greenhouses required additional heat if they were to successfully grow exotic plants, fruit and vegetables. Initially, coal was the fuel of choice and, as the century progressed, boiler designs and innovations led to increased heating efficiency.

Trade had already brought new and exotic plant species to our shores, but Britain's temperamental weather meant that alternative ways of replicating the sunnier climates they originated from had to be found. Heated greenhouses, or hot houses, became the latest addition to Victorian gardens, extending the array of fruit, vegetables and flowers that could be supplied for the dinner table. The hothouse was comprised of a section of pipework leading from a boiler to provide a dry heat, allowing rows upon rows of exotic plants to thrive during the cold winter months. To enhance the humid atmosphere enjoyed by some tropical varieties, water was regularly thrown on to the hot pipes to create steam. Greenhouses without heat were known as 'Cold Frames'.

Like the walled garden, the greenhouse/hothouse layout was well-planned. Soft fruits, such as peaches, might be grown in one area, with melon or cucumber in another. Some estates had multiple hothouses, allowing different varieties to be grown in each and ensuring that vigorous, rapidly growing plants did not overshadow their diminutive neighbours. It was not uncommon to have one hothouse set aside for melons, one for pineapples and one for grapevines, each specifically designed and maintained to enable the best conditions for the fruit.

The Perfect Pineapple

After discovering the pineapple in Guadaloupe in 1493, Christopher Columbus is famed for introducing the fruit to European cuisine. Extremely difficult to grow in our cooler climate, gardeners and horticulturists endlessly researched how best to cultivate this new exotic fruit. When King Charles II's gardener, John Rose, successfully grew a pineapple for the Royal table, the occasion was captured for posterity in a painting by Hendrick Danckerts in 1675. As a result, the English were inspired by its unique shape and form and took to using the pineapple symbol in many architectural elements and motifs. It appeared carved in stone on top of buildings, or mimicked in the shape of garden ornaments and planters. Such was its artistic appeal that it made the perfect statement piece, topping everything from bedposts and bookends, pottery finials and elaborate fountains.

The pineapple soon became the fruit of choice for the upper classes. A hostess's status in society was raised by her ability to present such an expensive fruit at dinner. Not only did the uniquely shaped fruit create a centrepiece within an ornate food display, but it was also associated with wealth and prosperity.

Victorian gardeners understood that the pineapple needed different methods of cultivation to prosper in colder climates. One method was to create a 'pineapple pit', consisting of three trenches covered in glass and positioned slightly below ground level, yet connected with two cavity walls. The outer trenches were filled with fresh horse manure which gave off heat during decomposition. The heat passed through small holes within the walls to the central cavity, where the pineapples were grown. This clever device required regular manual labour to ensure that fresh manure was constantly added into the outer cavities to maintain the warm temperature.

In 1993, an original pineapple pit was discovered and renovated in the Lost Gardens of Heligan, near Mevagissey in Cornwall; within four years, the first pineapple was successfully grown using this early technique.

Despite all the efforts of Victorian gardeners, it was still far easier to cultivate the exotic fruit in hot countries overseas. When steamships were introduced, shortening the journey times between trading countries, it became cheaper to transport the pineapples from abroad rather than to grow them in Britain.

Ice Houses

In 1619 James I commissioned the building of the first ice house in Greenwich Park, London. Engineered to regulate temperature, with their brick-lined walls and cylindrical shape, these seventeenth century ice stores were located near to water sources for easy storage of ice and snow after harvest from a lake or river in the depths of winter.

It was a cold and thankless job for the estate workers required to perform this task. To make doubly sure that their efforts were not wasted, they would also line the brick shaft of the construction with bales of straw to deter the ice from melting. By 1660, Charles II used his scientifically constructed ice house in Upper St James's Park to impress guests with its ability to provide chilled drinks and ices even in the summer months. It prompted the poet Edmund Waller to write:

> *Yonder the harvest of cold months laid up,*
> *Gives a fresh coolness to the Royal cup,*
> *There ice, like crystal, firm and never lost,*
> *Tempers hot July with December's Frost;*
> *Winter's dark prison, whence he cannot fly,*
> *Tho' the warm spring, his enemy draws nigh:*
> *Strange! That extremes should thus preserve the snow,*
> *High on the Alps or in the deep caves below.*

Although ice houses vary in design depending upon their date of construction, most were domed structures with a large proportion of their volume underground and worked by insulating the cold. Due to their locations under trees or away from the main house, their presence was not obvious and many still survive, hidden deep within the vegetation of a country estate. For decades they aided the storage of perishable goods and the preparation of chilled desserts such as ice creams and syllabubs for the upper classes, long before the ice trade revolutionised the way we preserve our food.

Those unable to afford a brick-built ice house would create 'snow stacks' by covering the gathered snow with thatch. Others chose the more convenient method of buying a block of ice from their fishmonger. Once delivered, it would be wrapped in sacking and placed in a metal-lined chest, which was used as an early refrigerator. Inside were a couple of shelves where food could be placed and kept cool. A tap on the bottom of the chest allowed any melted water to be drained away into a bowl beneath.

The first transatlantic ice cargo arrived in England from Wenham Lake in America in 1844. In temperatures below freezing the ice was harvested by a crew of men, using horse-drawn vehicles and cutting tools. The blocks were then hooked from the lake and slid onto sledges before being transported to ice houses on the shore.

It had been discovered that, if securely insulated, ice could last a long time before it began to melt. Sawdust proved to be the perfect insulator on the ships that brought lake ice to Britain. With the approval of Queen Victoria, the Wenham Lake Ice Company was awarded a royal warrant. The company mesmerised the public when it opened a shop front in the Strand in London and each day displayed a large block of ice in the window, with a newspaper propped behind it, so that passers-by could 'miraculously' read the print through the frozen water.

The Americans realised that ice could be used to chill drinks, create frozen desserts and even soothe medical complaints. The discovery that packing foodstuffs in ice enabled them to be transported and consumed far from where they were produced, paved the way for a whole variety of items to be sold to distant markets. Such was the British demand for this commodity, that vast quantities of this frozen water were sourced from North America and Norway.

Only the invention of the refrigerator at the end of the century marked the decline of the ice trade and the sad demise of the brick-lined ice houses, which lay abandoned forever in the corners of country estates.

Conclusion: Changing Times

The death of Queen Victoria in January 1901 marked the end of an era which had seen more changes and advancements than any other period in history. But it was also the start of a new century, and with it came more innovations and developments than the world had previously imagined possible. Edward VII continued the culinary standards set by his mother, but also introduced some new ideas of his own. He took a liking to French cuisine, and its tastes and methods were introduced into British kitchens and dining rooms in the form of truffles, patisseries and fine champagne, whilst employing a French chef – often paid handsomely for their skills and expertise – was considered the height of fashion.

For the wealthy, dining was extended outside the home, as luxury restaurants became the places to be seen. Each establishment offered sophisticated menus and only the best produce to complement the grand balls and supper parties held into the early hours of the morning. By day, they became elegant meeting places where people could stop for lunch or enjoy the added entertainment of a tea dance, and settings where respectable – and sometimes not so respectable – men and women could meet in civilised surroundings.

Forward-thinking and ambitious domestic servants saw the new restaurants as their way out of traditional service and took employment at these up-and-coming venues and hotels, giving them the chance to see the world from a different perspective. Life was changing at a rapid pace and the Edwardian era also signalled more freedom and opportunities for women. With openings in the growing number of factories and shops, the relentless drudgery of domestic service started to hold less and less appeal. Better pay and more time off attracted servants and their numbers gradually began to decrease.

A defining moment came with the outbreak of the First World War in 1914, which had a huge impact on the upkeep and operation of Britain's country houses. When a large proportion of their male workforce enrolled to do their bit for King and Country, the gentry found that they no longer had a houseful of servants to cater for their every whim. Death duties crippled many estates and some families no longer had the resources to keep their homes in the condition to which they were accustomed. Many were either sold off or fell into disrepair, while others were requisitioned for war work or as military hospitals, with dining rooms remodelled into makeshift nursing facilities and kitchens turning out food for patients rather than society guests.

Female domestics realised that they too could get involved, training as nurses, drivers and working the land. They filled many traditionally male roles and often enjoyed what was to be their first real taste of independence. Four years later, despite Britain's ultimate victory in Europe, life would never revert back to how it had been before the war. Few desired to return to domestic service. Women had witnessed a completely different world outside the confines of domestic life and could see new opportunities to broaden their horizons and a whole host of challenges to face in the years ahead.

The male workforce had changed, too. Although there was an influx of manpower when army, navy and air force personnel were demobbed, many of the jobs left by those who had gone to fight and never returned were no longer deemed necessary. Rail, road and steam transportation had made the world a smaller place, allowing foodstuffs to be shipped from further afield and maintaining the kitchen gardens of larger properties was no longer a priority.

Families were overjoyed if their husbands, fathers and sons returned from the conflict, but there was still a sense of loss for the women who had to step aside once more as the men took back the jobs that they had once carried out. The country houses they had worked in before the war no longer operated in the same way, and there was an undercurrent of resentment from those who found it difficult to return to its unique hierarchy after fighting on the front line. The lure, security and status of domestic service was rapidly dwindling and a complete way of life, which had once dominated working class British employment, was disappearing, never to be recovered again.

The upper classes felt the change too. The stalwarts dug their heels in, believing that life would eventually return to normal, but a new breed of gentry were eager to throw off the restraints of the war years and simply enjoy themselves during the 1920s, with clothes, hairstyles, cars and music changing dramatically from the confinements of the Edwardian and Victorian eras.

But the good life was short-lived and when World War Two broke out in 1939, the final nail was added to the coffin of domestic service. Lavish dinner parties were no longer held by the wealthy, where course after course of exquisitely prepared dishes were slaved over in kitchens across the country – there simply wasn't enough food to go around. An era of rationing impacted even on the rich, as basic items like butter, cheese, sugar and tea were now limited by weight and availability. Through it all the kitchen was a place of sanctuary where families could congregate as they learnt the fate of loved ones involved in the current conflict; a place where clothing was remodelled under the wartime ruling of 'Make Do and Mend'; and a place where friendships were forged, romances sealed and problems shared.

Despite the changing times, here in the kitchen nothing had changed. The housewife was still mistress of her domain, she was simply juggling different problems; still making ends meet and ultimately, trying to prepare something out of nothing to feed her family. The cycle continues to turn. No matter how modern we think our lives have become, we are influenced by the past and, for many of us, the kitchen remains the heart of our home.

Tracing Food Industry Forebears

Records relating to chefs, domestic cooks and kitchen maids are not always the easiest documents to find and researchers require diligence – and often a little luck – to track down details about their careers. But you may still be able to find information that could help you flesh out the working lives of those in the Victorian food industry or domestic service.

Where possible, try to locate the individual on the census and check back through each decade to establish how long they were employed in their position. Websites hosting British census records, like Ancestry. co.uk, Findmypast.co.uk or TheGenealogist.co.uk, should be able to help in the initial stages of your quest. The address given on the census could provide clues as to the type of place they worked in – a restaurant, country house, or institution. Bear in mind that many caterers and servants gained experience in a variety of workplaces – on board ships, or in military and school kitchens. Everyone needed to be fed, whether a patient in a hospital, or a duke and duchess at a fine hotel, and your ancestor may well have been the one with the skills to prepare and provide their meals.

The location of their workplace will determine your next port of call. Institutions like old hospitals, asylums and workhouses may no longer operate under their original purpose, but their staff records may have been deposited in the local history archives or record office. Get in touch to see what information they hold – the smallest snippet about an individual's role could be the key to understanding the rest of their career.

For those engaged in domestic service in a country house or grand mansion, contact the existing estate directly to enquire about past members of staff and employment records. Larger properties taken over by the National Trust or another heritage organisation will usually be happy to help and interested to know any extra details you may have about an ex-employee. If the kitchens have been restored for public display, then you may have the opportunity to see for yourself where your forebear once worked and the type of kitchen equipment in use at the time.

Perhaps the house no longer exists but was once a significant property within the community. In this case, contact the relevant county record office to see if estate papers, documents, letters and even household log books have been added to their holdings. Historical directories can enable you to find out where now lost country homes were situated. Examples of commercial, professional, general trade and national and provincial directories for individual years can be found at *www.historicaldirectories.org* or at *www.ancestry.co.uk* – those produced by Frederick Kelly and James Pigot are extremely useful – whilst the websites of individual repositories often have online help. Shropshire Records Office, for example, provides a downloadable guide on how to research alternative sources on domestic servant ancestors at: *www.shropshire.gov.uk/media/59138/24-servant-sources.pdf*.

Don't dismiss newspapers when tracking someone down. From chefs who worked in high-end restaurants to those who were employed in a local hotel, their culinary creations could well have made the headlines. Lavish banquets or dinners for visiting dignitaries could have been documented and the establishment staff may have been mentioned. Most people in catering can be highly competitive when it comes to producing a gastronomic masterpiece, so if you know that the individual you seek enjoyed a challenge, or have perhaps heard that they won awards, then turn to the newspapers for help.

Others found themselves the focus of media coverage for more negative reasons, like Alice Vokes, whose death was reported in the *Daily Gazette for Middlesbrough* on 21 August 1893:

On Saturday afternoon Dr J.S Walton, coroner, held an inquest at Bolton Hall, near Leyburn, on the body of Alice VOKES (33) cook. On Friday afternoon one of the kitchen maids of Bolton Hall, saw something fall past the kitchen window, and on going out, found that it was the deceased, who had fallen from her bedroom window, where she had been sitting. The jury returned an open verdict.

Even an obituary can hold clues about an individual's culinary past. Visit the local archives in the area where your ancestor was based to discover more. There are a wide variety of searchable historic newspapers online at the British Newspaper Archive (*www.britishnewspaperarchive.co.uk*) spanning the period from 1710 to 1965, including over 200 local titles. Don't forget that each county archive will also have a collection of local newspapers; copies on microfilm or original examples can provide fascinating glimpses of life during a specific era.

Wills, probate records and coroners' reports can all provide extra detail and help to link an individual to specific places of work or name their employers and work colleagues. For example, some domestics were so highly regarded by their employers that they received bequests after their deaths. Martin Ware made his will in July 1868 and in gratitude to his household staff for the work they carried out, he left small bequests to them all when he died four years later. A sizeable sum of £50 was left to his cook Harriet Canham, whose culinary skills he must have thoroughly enjoyed!

To be distributed among Farm Labourers at Tilford £25; To servant Mary Dibden an annuity of £25; To John Beagley gardener at Tilford an annuity of £10; To Harriet Canham, cook in London £50; To James Cage coachman in London, Thomas Beagley footman at Tilford and [...] Willis cook at Tilford 19 guineas; To bailiff Coppar £10; To rest of domestic servants in London and at Tilford £5.

The biggest clues, however, may lie in the possessions left behind by an individual and stored away with family ephemera, perhaps in a shoebox or suitcase in the attic. Take a good look at any letters for clues; hotel flyers and advertising leaflets from restaurants, could provide crucial lines of enquiry; newspaper clippings, old wage packets, photographs and family diaries are well worth examining in detail. A chance line written in a letter could lift the lid on a place or period of employment or even an unusual event.

Ask relatives to see if they have any kitchen items that have been handed down within the family. Now dated pieces of equipment were modern time-saving gadgets of their day and could be significant if someone thought they were worth keeping. By carefully examining these items you should be able to roughly date them to the period in which they were in use.

Finally, the Holy Grail of a cook's treasures would undoubtedly be their recipe book, where menus were planned, much-loved dishes documented and new ideas concocted. Notes in the margins and useful cuttings that were important to the writer are not only fascinating for getting a feel for the period, but also help you to build a bigger picture of the type of food they would have been producing at the time.

The stories surrounding the lives of those who worked hard to provide food and put meals on the tables of the Victorian population are endless; it is just a case of donning your detective hat and knowing where to look!

Genealogy Websites

Access to Archives – www.nationalarchives.gov.uk/a2a
Part of the UK archives network, the database contains catalogues detailing the archives held locally in England and Wales – ideal for pinpointing the resources available in your area.

Ancestry – www.ancestry.co.uk
A one-stop-shop of genealogical information. Discover domestic servant ancestors listed on birth, marriage and death records, track down their changing occupations on the census, or scour online directories, wills and probate records to find out more about their individual roles.

Findmypast – www.findmypast.co.uk
Another UK genealogy site providing a wealth of records to the researcher. As part of a long-term project to increase access to the information held in the Royal Archives, a selection of records relating to Royal Household employees have been made available on Findmypast. co.uk. These include payment and employment lists. It is also home to the British Newspaper Archive, an historical newspaper archive featuring examples from England, Scotland and Wales spanning the years 1710 to 1953 and including more than 200 local titles.

The Genealogist – www.thegenealogist.co.uk
With an ever-growing range of data sets, this genealogy website allows users to search by occupation to locate an individual. It holds extensive collections of peerage, heritage and landowner records, especially useful if you think your ancestor worked for the aristocracy.

The National Archives – www.nationalarchives.gov.uk
The official archive of the UK government.

Other Resources

The National Trust (*www.nationaltrust.org.uk*) and **English Heritage** (*www.english-heritage.org.uk*) websites are vital for discovering more about the individual collections held by some of Britain's most important stately homes, gardens, mills and monuments. Arrange a visit to an individual property to get a real insight into life in another era. For instance, at Audley End in Essex you can explore the kitchens where cook Avis Crocombe once worked and the restored kitchen garden where she would have sourced her fresh ingredients. The working estate of Shugborough Hall, now run by the National Trust, provides a glimpse into the world of the country house kitchen, as well as the farm where traditional skills would have been used to create butter and cheese.

More information on **Servant Tax Rolls for Scotland** can be found at the Royal Commission on the Ancient and Historical Monuments of Scotland website (*www.rcahms.gov.uk*).

Explore **Emma Darwin's Diaries**: The 60 volumes detailing her everyday life between 1824 and 1896, including her recipe books, are online, at: *http://darwin-online.org.uk/EmmaDiaries.html*

The Museum of London website (*www.museumoflondon.org.uk*) provides a fantastic online resource on shopping and eating habits during the Victorian era.

Queen Victoria's Household: Throughout her life, Queen Victoria was an avid journal writer, recording her thoughts, observations and feelings about daily events and family issues. The website *www.queen-victorias-scrapbook.org* draws upon some of the information from her diaries and personal correspondence, along with original source material and documents from the Royal Collections. Under the category 'Queen Victoria's Household' is a photograph of the Royal Kitchens at Windsor, dating from 1878. Although sepia in tone, the kitchen looks spotless, with the pans and kitchenware arranged as regimentedly as if they were awaiting an inspection from the monarch herself.

In 2002, **The Mills Archive** was established to create a permanent repository for historical and contemporary material on traditional mills and milling. The amount of information collected upon this subject is extremely appealing for the family and social historian. Over one million documents and images have been rescued, enabling us to fully understand more about those who worked in this trade or merely used their services on a daily basis. By searching the mill people database you can track down workers and establish the closest mill to your ancestor's home. Once discovered, it is fascinating to think that they would have relied upon the miller's services and bought his flour to bake bread for their family. Find out more at *www.millsarchivetrust.org*

The **Rural Museums Network** (*www.ruralmuseums.ssndevelopment. org*) brings together our rural heritage through museums which concentrate upon the history and traditions of farming and country life. This site is worth a visit if you wish to find out more about the day-to-day skills and techniques used by our ancestors. By providing links to English Heritage sites, archives, indexes and societies, it offers the ideal starting point from which to find out more about your particular area of interest.

Timeline

1837   Queen Victoria ascended the throne.

1839   Indian tea first became available in Britain. Previously only tea from China had been imported and the alternative helped to reduce the overall price.

1840   During this decade the first closed cooking ranges were introduced, with temperature-controlled systems following soon after.

1845   Eliza Acton published *Modern Cookery for Private Families.*

1845   Henry Jones of Bristol is credited with inventing self-raising flour between 1845 and 1853.

1845   Charles Elmé Francatelli published *The Modern Cook.*

1845   Potato blight leads to famine in Ireland.

1846   Repeal of the Corn Laws.

1847   Fry & Son produced the first chocolate bar, made from cocoa powder, sugar and melted cocoa butter extracted from cocoa beans. By 1875, milk had been added to the mix to make the first milk chocolate bar.

1850s The introduction of the railways soon enabled food to be transported quickly around the country.

1851   Catherine Dickens published a selection of menus under the title of *What Shall We Have for Dinner?* using the pseudonym of Lady Maria Clutterbuck.

1851   Along with a myriad of new inventions, the first gas ovens were exhibited at the Great Exhibition at Crystal Palace, although they were not popular until the 1890s as people worried about the risk of explosion.

1855   Bread riots took place in Liverpool as bakers and other food shops were looted by the starving poor.

1855   Alexis Soyer wrote *A Shilling Cookery Book for the People.*

1856   Louis Pasteur discovered how to make milk safer by killing bacteria through his pasteurisation process.

1858   John Lees opened the first fish and chip shop in Oldham.

1860   The first British Food and Drugs Act was passed to prevent harmful additives being used in food manufacture.

1861   Mrs Beeton's *Book of Household Management* was published.

1865   The first large-scale canning factory was set up by the Admiralty to can meat to feed the soldiers and sailors across the Empire.

1885   Agnes Bertha Marshall, known as Queen of the Ices, published *Ices Plain and Fancy: The Book of Ices*, the first of four cookery books she was to produce.

1891   Crompton and Co were the first British firm to invent the electric kettle.

1901   The death of Queen Victoria marks the end of an era.

1903   Sainsbury's starts selling tea, coffee, sugar and other groceries.

Bibliography

Acton, Eliza, *Modern Cookery for Private Families* (1845).

Adams, Samuel; Adams, Sarah, *The Complete Servant* (1825).

Arch, Joseph, *Stories of His Life Told by Himself*, (Hutchinson,1898).

Bailey Catherine, *Black Diamonds – The Rise and Fall of an English Dynasty*, (Viking, 2007).

Beecher Stowe, Harriet, *Uncle Tom's Cabin; or Life Among the Lowly* (1852).

Beeton, Isabella, *Mrs Beeton's Book of Household Management* (1861).

Briffault, Eugene, *Paris à Table* (1846).

Carroll, Lewis, *Alice in Wonderland* (1865).

Cassell's *Dictionary of Cookery* (1875).

Colquhoun, Kate, *A Thing in Disguise: The Visionary Life of Joseph Paxton*, (Harper Perennial, 2009).

Cowen, Ruth, *Relish: The Extraordinary Life of Alexis Soyer, Victorian Celebrity Chef* (Orion, 2010 edition).

Cullwick, Hannah; Stanley, Elizabeth ed., *The Diaries of Hannah Cullwick* (Virago Press, 1984).

Davies, Jennifer, *The Victorian Country Kitchen* (BBC Books, 1989).

De-la-Noy, Michael, *Queen Victoria at Home*, (De Capo Press 2005).

Denyer, Susan, *Beatrix Potter: At Home in the Lake District*, (Frances Lincoln, 2000).

Dickens, Catherine, *What Shall We Have for Dinner?* (1851).

Dickens, Charles, *A Christmas Carol* (1843).

—— *Oliver Twist* (1837-9)

—— *The Pickwick Papers* (1836-7).

Dickens, Charles; Evans, Frederic, *Dickens's Dictionary of London: An Unconventional Guide* (1879).

Dickson Wright, Clarissa, *A History of English Food*, (Arrow, 2012).

Forrester, Mark, *Forrester's Pictorial Miscellany* (1855).

Fuller, William, *A Manual Concerning Numerous Original Recipes for Preparing Neapolitan Ices* (1855).

Green, Percy B., *History of Nursery Rhymes* (1899).

Hardy, Thomas, *Jude the Obscure* (1895).

Henry Baylis, T., *The Rights, Duties and Relations of Domestic Servants and Their Masters* (1857).

Horn, Pamela, *The Rise and Fall of the Victorian Servant* (Sutton Publishing, 1986).

Jermy, Louise, *Memoirs of a Working Woman* (1934).

Kemp, Philip Robert, *The Dictionary of Daily Wants* (Houlston & Wright, 1859).

Kibble Hervey, Thomas, *The Book of Christmas* (1836).

Kitchener, William, *The Housekeeper's Oracle* (1829).

Marsh, Jan, *William Morris and Red House: A Collaboration between Architect and Owner* (National Trust Books, 2005).

Mayhew, Henry, *London Labour and the London Poor*, volumes 1-3, (1851).

Moore, George, *Esther Walters* (1894).

Musson, Jeremy, *Up and Down Stairs – The History of the Country House Servant*, (John Murray, 2010).

Paterson, Michael, *Private Life in Britain's Stately Homes* (2012).

Pethick-Lawrence, Emmeline, *My Part in a Changing World* (1938).

Powell, Margaret, *Below Stairs* (Thorndike Press, 2013 edition).

Robert Malcolmson, R., and Mastoris, S., *The English Pig: A History*, (Continuum, 2003).

Sims, George, *Horrible London* (Billing and Sons, 1889).

Soyer, A., *The Modern Housewife* (1851).

—— *A Shilling Cookery Book for the People*, (1855).

Thackeray, W. M., *Complete Works* (1899).

—— *Pendennis* (1848).

Thompson, F., *Lark Rise to Candleford* (1939).

Timbs, John, *Curiosities of London* (1867).

Walker, Harlan, *Cooks and Other People* (Prospect Books, 1996).

Wells, Robert, *The Bread & Biscuit Bakers & Sugar Boiler's Assistant* (1890).

Yorke, T., *Country House Explained (England's Living History)*, (Countryside Books, 2003).

Newspapers and Journals

The English Woman's Domestic Magazine
The Girl's Own Paper
The Illustrated London News
Leisure Hour
The Morning Chronicle
The Penny Magazine
The Stamford Mercury
The Times
The Weekly Post

Index